# The Changing Pattern of Employment

This title, first published in 1973, covers the period of 1959 to 1968. The study suggests that government policies had very little effect on the employment structures of the sub-regions at this time, despite government intervention and policy objectives in Great Britain to reduce levels of unemployment in the depressed regions and curb congestion in the Midland and South East England conurbations. Instead, regional employment structures seemed to be determined by what was happening to industries at a national level.

This study will be of interest to economists, planners, regional scientists and geographers, as well as students in these fields.

# The Changing Pattern of Employment

## of Employment

Regional Specialisation and
Industrial Localisation in
Britain

**Michael Chisholm
Jim Oeppen**

Routledge
Taylor & Francis Group

First published in 1973
by Croom Helm

This edition first published in 2016 by Routledge
2 Park Square, Milton Park, Abingdon, Oxon, OX14 4RN
and by Routledge
711 Third Avenue, New York, NY 10017

*Routledge is an imprint of the Taylor & Francis Group, an informa business*

© 1973 M. Chisholm and J. Oeppen

**Publisher's Note**
The publisher has gone to great lengths to ensure the quality of this reprint but points out that some imperfections in the original copies may be apparent.

**Disclaimer**
The publisher has made every effort to trace copyright holders and welcomes correspondence from those they have been unable to contact.

A Library of Congress record exists under LC control number: 74166940


ISBN 13: 978-1-138-95651-3 (hbk)
ISBN 13: 978-1-315-66570-2 (ebk)

Michael Chisholm and Jim Oeppen

# The Changing Pattern of Employment

Regional Specialisation and Industrial Localisation in Britain

CROOM HELM LONDON

First published 1973
© 1973 by M. Chisholm and J. Oeppen

Croom Helm Ltd, 2–10 St Johns Road, London SW 11

ISBN 0-85664-022-0

Printed in Great Britain
by Ebenezer Baylis & Son Ltd
The Trinity Press, Worcester, and London
bound by G. & J. Kitcat Ltd, London

# Contents

# List of Tables

# List of Figures

# Preface

The work reported in this book started as a research project in which Professor Gordon Cameron, at the University of Glasgow, was closely involved. Indeed, he played a major part in setting up the enterprise and in arranging for data to be prepared for computer-based manipulation. Though it was not possible for him to maintain a close association with the work as it progressed, we are nevertheless very much in his debt. Mr Alan Ferguson, a graduate student at Bristol, also made numerous helpful suggestions and the illustrations were drawn by Mr Simon Godden, Department of Geography, University of Bristol. We also wish to acknowledge the generous grant made by the Nuffield Foundation to cover the salary of Mr Jim Oeppen for somewhat over a year while he worked full-time preparing and analysing data and also to cover incidental expenses. Without this grant, the work could not have been done.

M.C.
J.O.

# A note of explanation

In this study, we have used the 152 Minimum List industries
defined for statistical purposes. These all have their own three-
figure code number. For purposes of computation and analysis,
we have assigned these industries our own code, ranging from 1 to
152 (see Appendix). In the text, where there is the possibility of
confusing these two codes, the following convention has been
used. Reference to industry *120* (MLH 701), for example, is a
reference to MLH industry 701 to which we have assigned our
own code of 120.

The correct description of these MLH classes is 'category
of employment'. This is a clumsy phrase and we have frequently
used the much briefer term 'industry'. When used without
qualification, the term industry is synonymous with category of
employment and carries no connotation regarding the nature of
that employment.

# Chapter 1 Introduction

The post-war period has witnessed considerable interest in the spatial allocation of resources and, though government intervention has varied both in the means employed and the vigour of execution, the degree of government involvement has undoubtedly increased over the past two decades. In the immediate post-war period of Labour government, there was an active policy of regional assistance but this wavered and faded out of sight during the Conservative administrations of the 1950s. Indeed, by the early 1960s, it was widely felt that the 'regional problem' had been solved. However, with economic stagnation, even depression, in 1962 and 1963, there was a marked re-awakening of interest in problems of regional development (Chisholm, 1962) and the advent of a Labour administration in 1964 gave great impetus to this change. The following five or six years saw a veritable flood of legislation directed towards correcting regional imbalance (McCrone, 1969). In 1970, when a Conservative administration was returned to power, it appeared that the tempo of legislative change would slacken. In the event, the first years of the 1970s have seen plenty of changes and it is clear that whatever the political colour of the government, there will be a continuing commitment to active intervention in the spatial allocation of resources (see Chisholm and Manners, 1971).

At no time have the policy objectives of regional intervention been spelled out with great precision but two main intentions can be identified. The first has been the abiding concern to reduce the levels of unemployment in Ulster, Scotland, parts of northern England and elsewhere to something nearer the national average. Regional and intra-regional differences in unemployment rates have been remarkably persistent throughout the post-war period and these differences are rightly regarded as both socially unjust and economically wasteful. The second main reason for an interest in regional development lies in the problems of congestion, etc., arising from the previously uncontrolled growth of the conurbations in general and of London and Birmingham in particular. Strenuous

11

efforts have been made to limit the growth of employment in these two conurbations.

In pursuit of the first objective, two main strategies have been employed, both predicated on the general assumption that it is better to stimulate employment in areas with a large proportion of the workforce out of work than to encourage migration from these areas to places where the demand for labour is chronically in excess of the supply. While there is dispute about the precise importance of structural changes in the economy as a cause of spatial variations in unemployment levels, there can be no doubt whatever that the run-down of employment in certain industries has been of major importance. Coal mining, cotton textiles and ship-building are perhaps the three most familiar industries in this context (but see Chap. 5). In each case, special provision has been made to reduce the rate of decline. The coal industry has been protected by a tax on fuel oil, restrictions on coal imports and pressure on the Central Electricity Generating Board to use coal in preference to other fuels, notably oil. Cotton textiles have been helped by massive subsidies for re-equipment and by import quotas. In the case of shipbuilding, aid has been forthcoming in the form of special investment incentives, by the placement of government orders for naval vessels and as special aid for the restructuring of the industry on the Clyde.

If the effect of these and similar policies has been to reduce the rate at which regional economies have had to experience adjustments in their employment structure, another group of policies has had precisely the opposite effect. With varying degrees of vigour, post-war governments have taken positive steps to discourage the growth of employment in the London-Midlands part of the country and to steer expansion into the less fortunate regions, variously designated as Development Districts, Development Areas, Intermediate Areas, etc. In pursuit of this purpose, two categories of policy are to be noted. The first is general inducements, such as investment grants and the Regional Employment Premium, for which 'indigenous' and 'immigrant' firms are equally eligible within the defined geographical areas. The second category is the use of powers to encourage firms to move from one part of the country to another: the main instrument is the machinery governing the award of Industrial Development Certificates but the process has also been aided by the building of

12

advance factories, special housing provision for key workers, etc. In recent years, employment in offices has been subject to controls similar to those applied to manufacturing industry, with the aim of decentralising office work from London and Birmingham in particular.

The main purpose of policy measures to affect the geographical distribution of employment through IDCs, etc., has been to increase the aggregate number of jobs in the less fortunate areas. However, the means for achieving this imply the introduction of industries new to the less fortunate regions, or the fostering of industries which are under-represented. Consequently, it is to be expected that in the areas of high unemployment the policies pursued by government should have had a marked impact on the employment structure—and in general toward the diversification of job opportunities, as new industries replace the jobs lost through the run-down of traditional staple industries like coal-mining and textiles.

Evidence collected by Howard (1968) relating to mobile *manufacturing* plants in the period 1945 to 1965 certainly yields material to suggest that mobile industry ought to have had a quite detectable impact on the employment structure of some regions (Table 1.1). The eleven standard regions covering the United Kingdom fall into three fairly well-defined groups. At the top of the table are four regions, where the flow of immigrant firms has generated employment far in excess of that lost by the out-migration of plants and on a scale to make a large impact on the regional economies. Four other regions occupy the bottom of the table, with out-moves exceeding the importance of in-moves, though to an extent less marked than in the case of the first group. Finally, the middle group of three regions experienced a moderate excess of in-movement over out-movement.

Now, if the mobile plants were distributed among the industrial classes in such a way that the structure of in-moves and out-moves for each region exactly matched the stock of industries in the respective regions, then no change in industrial structure would occur. However, this is not only an inherently implausible proposition but is clearly refuted by the evidence in Table 1.2, showing that nationally the structure of mobile industry is very different from the structure of total industrial employment. Therefore, we may conclude that the movement of manufacturing

**Table 1.1** United Kingdom: employment in manufacturing plants mobile during the period 1945–1965 as a percentage of total industrial employment, 1966, by regions.

| Standard region | Inter-regional moves to region | Inter-regional moves originating in region | Total employment, mid-1966 |
|---|---|---|---|
| | % | % | 000 |
| Wales | 28·7 | 2·6 | 326 |
| Northern Ireland | 21·3 | — | 187 |
| North | 19·6 | 1·1 | 458 |
| Scotland | 12·8 | 0·7 | 740 |
| South West | 9·1 | 2·7 | 408 |
| East Anglia | 8·9 | 5·7 | 188 |
| North West | 7·7 | 2·1 | 1,364 |
| East Midlands | 4·3 | 5·0 | 623 |
| Yorks & Humberside | 3·5 | 4·8 | 897 |
| South East | 1·2 | 8·5 | 2,603 |
| West Midlands | 0·7 | 7·4 | 1,259 |

Source: Howard, 1968, p.9

plants from one region to another is likely to cause changes in the distribution of employment within the standard regions to an extent closely associated with the magnitude of the excess or deficit of in-moves over out-moves.

This idea can be explored somewhat further on the basis of Howard's data. Employment at the end of 1966 in mobile plants is analysed by the twenty-four SIC Orders for three groups of standard region, as

$X_1$    South East and East Anglia
$X_2$    West Midlands, East Midlands, Yorkshire and Humberside, North West (excluding Merseyside) and South West (excluding Devon and Cornwall)
$X_3$    Northern Ireland, Scotland, Wales and North, plus areas excluded under $X_2$.

In Howard's terminology, $X_3$ represents the 'peripheral' regions that have been given special assistance. Taking the inwardly mobile

14

**Table 1.2**  United Kingdom: employment in manufacturing plants mobile during the period 1945–1965 as a percentage of total employment, 1966, by SIC industries.

| Industry | | Employees, 1966 | Employment in mobile plants, 1966 | Mobile employment as % of total for the industry |
|---|---|---|---|---|
| | | 000 | 000 | |
| XVI | 'Other' manufacturing industries | 343 | 52·6 | 15·4 |
| VI | Engineering and electrical goods | 2,338 | 344·8 | 14·7 |
| VIII | Vehicles | 833 | 105·6 | 12·7 |
| IV | Chemicals and allied industries | 528 | 62·5 | 11·8 |
| XII | Clothing and footwear | 544 | 62·6 | 11·5 |
| IX | Metal goods n.e.s. | 588 | 41·1 | 7·0 |
| X | Textiles | 796 | 53·9 | 6·8 |
| III | Food, drink and tobacco | 854 | 57·6 | 6·7 |
| XIII | Bricks, pottery, glass, cement, etc. | 348 | 22·4 | 6·4 |
| XV | Paper, printing and publishing | 650 | 31·3 | 4·8 |
| XIV | Timber, furniture, etc. | 290 | 13·8 | 4·8 |
| XI | Leather, leather goods and fur | 58 | 2·5 | 4·3 |
| V | Metal manufacture | 612 | 18·3 | 3·0 |
| VII | Shipbuilding and marine engineering | 215 | 1·1 | 0·5 |

Source: Howard, 1968, p.25

employment in the fourteen SIC classes that cover the manufacturing sector, pairwise correlations between the three areas yields the following levels of $r^2$:

$X_1$ on $X_2$ $\quad\quad r^2 = 0.780 \quad\quad\quad F = 31.983$
$X_1$ on $X_3$ $\quad\quad r^2 = 0.915 \quad\quad\quad F = 96.755$
$X_2$ on $X_3$ $\quad\quad r^2 = 0.911 \quad\quad\quad F = 92.465$

These results, all significant at the 99 per cent level, show that the structure of employment generated by mobile firms moving into the three areas is very similar. Perhaps more interesting is the fact that $X_3$ correlates more highly with both $X_1$ and $X_2$ than does $X_1$ with $X_2$.

On the other hand, the structure of the industrial base varies quite substantially from region to region. Thus, while one would expect the mobile industries to reflect the structure of the exporting areas, it is likely that the importing areas will find the incoming industry to differ in character from that which is already located there. The result would be spatially differentiated changes in industrial structure.

Table 1.3 lists the employment in the SIC industrial classes on a geographical basis comparable to that used by Howard, for the year 1959. This year has been chosen because it marks the start of our study period (see Chapter 2) and because, having data by Employment Exchange areas, it is reasonably easy to obtain totals by the geographical regions used by Howard. With these data, it is a simple matter to compare the structure of incoming employment ($X_1$, $X_2$ and $X_3$) with the structure of the employment stock (respectively $X_4$, $X_5$ and $X_6$). The results of these regressions are:

| | | |
|---|---|---|
| $X_1$ on $X_4$ | $r^2 = 0.890$ | $F = 97.092$ |
| $X_2$ on $X_5$ | $r^2 = 0.639$ | $F = 21.240$ |
| $X_3$ on $X_6$ | $r^2 = 0.123$ | $F = 1.680$ |

In the first two cases, the associations are significant at the 99 per cent level, whereas in the third case the result is not significant even at the 95 per cent level. The implication is clear. For the peripheral regions as defined by Howard, the structure of incoming mobile manufacturing employment is unlike the stock of existing manufacturing employment. With both the other regions, but especially that comprising the South East and East Anglia, the inflow of employment has had relatively little effect in changing the structure of employment.

The evidence just cited has two main weaknesses. It is based on the Main Order classes, and for manufacturing only. Changes occurring at the Minimum List level may either confirm or contradict these findings. In the second place, to compare the structure of employment generated by plants mobile over the period 1945–65 with the stock of employment in 1959 contains a potentially serious problem. The structure as of 1959 will have been affected by moves prior to that date. It follows that the lack of relationship between the employment generated by immigrant firms and the total stock of manufacturing employment in the peripheral regions understates the differences between the two populations of employed persons. Furthermore, this understatement of the difference is apparent despite the fact that, prior to 1959, government was actively encouraging industry to go to the Development Areas. Thus, it is a clear inference that government policy has indeed contributed to regionally differentiated shifts in employment structure.

16

**Table 1.3** Employment in SIC manufacturing industries in three areas of the United Kingdom, 1959.

| Industry | South East and East Anglia $X_4$ | Southern and midland England $X_5$ | Peripheral areas $X_6$ |
|---|---|---|---|
| III | 266,155 | 300,262 | 211,266 |
| IV | 169,087 | 173,923 | 162,046 |
| V | 52,832 | 323,470 | 206,338 |
| VI | 768,870 | 789,568 | 358,250 |
| VII | 59,932 | 27,456 | 190,473 |
| VIII | 292,443 | 479,568 | 83,840 |
| IX | 115,491 | 321,744 | 73,544 |
| X | 43,256 | 648,852 | 259,903 |
| XI | 22,219 | 29,123 | 8,579 |
| XII | 187,045 | 276,355 | 58,574 |
| XIII | 88,074 | 182,976 | 35,098 |
| XIV | 134,603 | 93,071 | 39,309 |
| XV | 295,231 | 173,985 | 78,309 |
| XVI | 112,457 | 118,193 | 65,489 |

Note: regions correspond to Howard, 1968, Appendices G, H and I: see p.14. For the meaning of $X_4$, $X_5$ and $X_6$, see p.16.

If the evidence regarding mobile industry leads one to expect that spatially differentiated shifts in industrial structure are occurring, it is important to remember that manufacturing accounts for only one-third of all civil employment. The primary industries have experienced a general decline in employment and, in the case of coal mining in particular, this decline has been located in limited geographical areas. To the extent that government policies have tried to off-set the loss of mining employment in the coalfield areas by fostering industrial development, the structure of total employment should have undergone an even more radical change than in the manufacturing sector alone. Thus, policies to replace jobs in the mines and other basic industries imply strongly differentiated geographical shifts in industrial structure.

By now, the reader will have realised the direction that the argument is taking and it is convenient at this juncture to put the main proposition baldly and then to engage in a brief recapitulation of history and of the work published by other scholars that bears upon the issue. The bald proposition is that during the nineteenth century there developed a high degree of regional specialisation as a concomitant of the localisation of industries (Smith, 1949), but that in the present century several factors have conspired to reduce the level of employment specialisation in many, if not most, parts of the country. The highly differentiated pattern was maintained up to the first world war and even through much of the inter-war period, though by the 1930s structural adaptation of the economy was beginning to blur some of the regional distinctions, but only marginally. Since the second world war, however, not only has the structural change gained momentum, but policies have been actively implemented with the avowed aim of diversifying the economies of the less fortunate regions.

Although in the 1930s there was a considerable discussion of diversification as a means for reducing unemployment in the depressed areas, the classical doctrines of economic thought—the idea of comparative advantage in the theory of international trade, theories of the location of industry and of large scale production —all pointed toward regional specialisation as a means to economic efficiency. As Tress pointed out, diversification as an aim of policy was not a respectable proposition within these terms of reference. 'But if employment is made an end for economic activity as well as efficiency, then it is equally relevant for the studies of the economist, and a diversification policy whose criterion is employment cannot be disregarded in a theory of industrial location' (Tress, 1938, p.141).

The Royal Commission under the Chairmanship of Sir Montague Barlow (Royal Commission, 1940), charged with the task of examining what policies government should adopt regarding the distribution of the industrial population, came to two conclusions relevant in the present context. First, government should intervene to affect the spatial distribution of population and employment. Secondly, that one aim of such intervention should be the:

> Encouragement of a reasonable balance of industrial development, so far as possible, throughout the various divisions or regions of Great Britain, coupled with appropriate diversification of industry in each division or region throughout the country. (Royal Commission, 1940, p.206).

18

Regional diversification was seen to be both the logical consequence of getting new kinds of employment into the depressed areas and a desirable goal in its own right, as a means of reducing the risks of future unemployment heavily concentrated in a few unfortunate areas. Since 1940, it has been generally accepted by all the administrations, whether Coalition, Conservative or Labour, that regional diversification of employment is both a proper and an important aim of policy in the fight against unemployment.

Though regional diversification was originally conceived primarily as a means for reducing unemployment and of limiting the future hazards arising from spatially concentrated declining industries, there are two other aspects of diversification to note. In the first place, some researchers have held that the degree of diversification is positively related to the long-term rate of growth of regions. For example, Keeble and Hauser have recently (1971 and 1972) examined the effect of specialised employment structures on the rates of growth, as measured by various economic indicators, for sub-regions in south-east England. They used an index of specialisation calculated for each area as follows:

$$I = \sqrt{P_1^2 + P_2^2 + \ldots\ldots P_n^2}$$

where I is the index of specialisation and $P_1$, $P_2$, ......$P_n$ are the percentages of employment in the industry classes. This index was calculated for twenty-two industry classes. They found that the degree of specialisation so measured

'is particularly important in that it is the only [independent variable] to appear in exactly the same form in all the main dependent variable results. This clearly indicates that areas which have specialised on particular industries, even in the growth region of South-East England, are especially vulnerable to absolute or relative decline.' (Keeble and Hauser, 1972, p. 29.)

This result, based upon multiple regression analysis in which growth proved to be negatively related to the degree of specialisation, accords with the findings of some other workers whom the authors quote but, as they also note, conflicts with other results. In particular, Britton (1967) found that in the Bristol region faster growth appeared to be associated with greater specialisation of the sub-regional economies. That there is conflict of testimony regarding the significance of specialisation *per se* for the rate of regional or sub-regional growth need occasion no surprise when it is reflected that, if other things are equal, a high degree of specialisation may be associated with *either* fast or slow growth, whereas a diverse economy is more likely to grow at an average rate. Apparently conflicting results, therefore, may arise if different workers use only a small sample of the nation's sub-regions.

Another reason why the study of specialisation and diversification is of considerable interest concerns the question of cyclical stability or instability of employment. Thompson (1965) hypothesised that cyclical instability of a city's economy is related to the total population in the manner shown in Figure 1.1. His proposition was that very small cities straddle the range from very stable to very unstable economies but that as city size increases there is a convergence of behaviour toward the mean. Thus, cities lie within the envelope curves. The reasoning behind this proposition is clear:

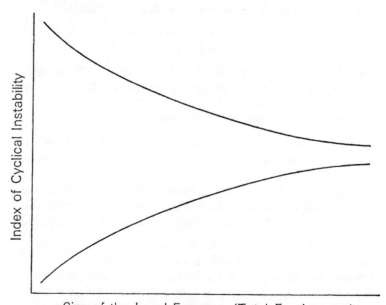

Size of the Local Economy (Total Employment)

Fig. 1.1    Schematic representation of the limits of cyclical instability related to city size.

Large urban economies tend to have diversified industrial structures and, therefore, tend to replicate the national degree of cyclical instability; the smaller urban economies exhibit a much greater range of cyclical instability by virtue of their heavier specialisation, in both the more unstable and the more stable industries. (Thompson, 1965, p.466).

Thompson was not able to pursue this hypothesis and test it empirically, though there is evidence that gives it good support at the national level (Chisholm, 1970). The limited amount of work done on local economic instability in Britain (Bassett and Haggett, 1971; Sant, 1971), using variations in unemployment at the Employment Exchange level, does not permit any firm conclusion to be drawn regarding the validity or otherwise of Thompson's hypothesis, though the evidence in Table 1.4 is highly suggestive that his thesis ought to be correct.

In the present study, no attempt will be made to measure cyclical instability. On the other hand, it is possible to examine a crucial step in the chain of reasoning—that the smaller an area's total employment, the more specialised the employment structure, and vice versa. This, therefore, represents the second main question to which we address ourselves.

Finally, there is of course the reverse side of the coin to consider. Changes in the degree of local specialisation may arise from either one or both of two processes. In the first place, individual industries may be becoming less highly localised, which would imply that each area has a more even mix of employment. Alternatively, if each industry remains highly localised, or indeed becomes more localised still, it is conceivable that local economies can nevertheless become more diversified. The nature of such a possible process is indicated by the imaginary employment data in Table 1.5, for three industries distributed among five zones. Between time t and t+1, industry I becomes more highly localised. At the same time, industry II retains the same degree of localisation but changes its geographical distribution, while industry III maintains precisely the same distribution. Looking across the rows, it is immediately evident that zones 1 to 4 inclusive have experienced an increase in diversification; only in the case of zone 5 has employment become more dependent upon one industry.

21

**Table 1.4**  Great Britain: average cyclical amplitudes in percentage unemployment, 1951–1966, by industry.

| Industry, SIC Order | Mean amplitude, % |
| --- | --- |
| Professional services | 0·3 |
| Mining and quarrying | 0·3 |
| Insurance, banking and finance | 0·4 |
| Gas, electricity and water | 0·4 |
| Paper, printing and publishing | 0·4 |
| Vehicles | 0·4 |
| Public administration and defence | 0·5 |
| Chemicals | 0·5 |
| Transport and communication | 0·6 |
| Engineering and electrical goods | 0·6 |
| Agriculture, forestry and fishing | 0·8 |
| Distributive trades | 0·8 |
| Metal manufacture | 0·9 |
| Textiles | 0·9 |
| Food, drink and tobacco | 0·9 |
| 'Other' manufacturing industries | 0·9 |
| Metal goods, n.e.s. | 0·9 |
| Leather, leather goods and fur | 0·9 |
| Timber, furniture, etc. | 0.9 |
| Bricks, pottery, glass, cement, etc. | 0·9 |
| Clothing and footwear | 1·0 |
| Miscellaneous services | 1·1 |
| Shipbuilding and marine engineering | 1·9 |
| Construction | 2·6 |

Source: Sant, 1971, p. 185.

Changes in the localisation of industries may be related to three main variables. In the first place, some industries have been more affected by government intervention than others, through the control of Industrial Development Certificates, investment incentives and other measures. Secondly, industries that have enjoyed rapid growth may have experienced major changes in their geographical distribution, partly because growth industries are those which generate investment proposals that are affected by government policies. Thirdly, and working in the opposite direction, industries subject to rapid contraction may also experience

**Table 1.5** Hypothetical data showing increasing regional diversification of employment with an increase in industrial localisation.

| Industry | Time t | | | | Time t + 1 | | | |
|---|---|---|---|---|---|---|---|---|
| | I | II | III | Total | I | II | III | Total |
| Zone 1 | 100 | 10 | 10 | 120 | 120 | 100 | 10 | 230 |
| 2 | 50 | 100 | 10 | 160 | 30 | 20 | 10 | 60 |
| 3 | 20 | 50 | 5 | 75 | 10 | 10 | 5 | 25 |
| 4 | 200 | 10 | 10 | 220 | 220 | 50 | 10 | 280 |
| 5 | 20 | 20 | 200 | 240 | 10 | 10 | 200 | 220 |
| Total | 390 | 190 | 235 | 815 | 390 | 190 | 235 | 815 |

substantial changes in their geographical distribution, especially if the decline is concentrated on specific sub-sectors that are themselves highly localised. On *a priori* grounds, there are no means of predicting the relative strengths of these tendencies and it is clearly necessary, therefore, to examine what has in fact been happening.

To conclude this section, then, the main point to be noted is that since the depression years of the 1930s successive governments have attempted to off-set the effects of secular decline in localised industries by introducing new employment into these areas. While the chief purpose has been to reduce the level of unemployment, pursuit of this goal should have resulted in spatially differentiated changes in the degree of specialisation of local economies. If this proposition is in fact true, then it should be possible to find clear evidence in its support: it is this quest that forms one of the main purposes of the present enquiry. This quest is undertaken in the light of the fact that the 'analysis of the development of industrial diversification . . . [is] one of the most neglected areas of study in sociology and economics' (Clemente and Sturgis, 1971, p.65). Geographers have given the subject equally little attention.

### Previous work on regional specialisation in Britain.

In this section, we briefly review previous work analysing changes over time in the degree of regional specialisation. The purpose here is to assemble such evidence as already exists bearing upon the main proposition made in the previous section.

Thus, attention focuses upon work relating to Britain and, furthermore, work that specifically reports changes over time, as against static analyses of the spatial distribution of specialisation/diversification within an area at one point in time (as for example Davies and Hagger, 1964; South East Economic Planning Council, 1970). In this section, the purpose is to report substantive findings and not to discuss methodological issues, which are reserved to Chapter 2.

Tress (1938) devised a statistic to measure the diversity of employment in an area, based on the following reasoning. Any one area has a given number of industries; the employment in each industry can be expressed as a percentage of the total employment in the area. These percentages can be ranked from highest to lowest and then successively added. The sum of the accumulated percentages will be greatest when the industrial employment is heavily concentrated into a few classes, and least when uniformly distributed among the N industrial classes. (For a full discussion of the method, see pp.31–2). Tress applied this technique to a sample of fourteen towns in England and Wales, using census data for 1931 and Ministry of Labour employment records for 1937. The fourteen towns were selected as ones suffering heavy unemployment and also displaying a highly specialised employment structure. On the basis of eighty-five classes of manufacturing industry, Tress found that in ten cases there had been some decrease in specialisation, in two no change and that for Barrow-in-Furness and Darlington there had even been a slight accentuation of the concentration of employment. Overall, a modest move to greater diversity of employment was evident in places such as Swansea, Rochdale and Bolton, for example.

Another way of looking at regional specialisation derives from Sargant Florence's (1944) concept of location quotients, a concept applicable to the location of an individual industry in a particular region. The location quotient for any industry (I) in any region (J) is obtained from the following expression:

Number employed in industry I in region J, as a percentage of the national total for that industry

---

Number employed in all industries in region J, as a percentage of the national total employment for all industries.

A ratio in excess of 1.0 implies that an industry is more highly localised in the region than is employment generally. Hall applied this technique to the industries of London, using census data for 1861 and 1951 (Hall, 1962). The high location quotients in 1951 were in general substantially less than the high values of 1861: for eleven industries in 1951, the median quotient was 1.8, compared with a median value (for ten industries) of 2.8 ninety years previously. He commented that for these London industries:

> Almost every manufacturing industry. . . . . . . . has a lower location quotient in 1951 than in 1861. This is characteristic of a tendency, not only for Greater London but for all regions of the country, to approach more closely in industrial structure to the national average. (Hall, 1962, p.26).

Hall went on to remark that W. Smith (1953, p.177) had noted a similar tendency in the Merseyside region. In a later study of this north-western conurbation, Lloyd (1970) found that relatively little change occurred in the employment structure between 1950 and 1958, whereas the period 1960 to 1967 saw a dramatic acceleration in the tempo of structural adaptation—notably, of course, with the arrival of car manufacturing on a large scale.

Florence (1944) also devised a coefficient of localisation, which can be derived for individual industries. Imagine any one industry distributed among several regions: the percentage employment in each region can be readily obtained. These percentages for the one industry can be compared with the equivalent array of percentages for total employment. If the positive differences between the percentage for industry and for all employment are obtained, and these are summed and divided by 100, an index is yielded with the following property. If the spatial distribution of the industry is identical to that of all employment, the index will be 0·0. On the other hand, if the industry is located entirely in one region, the coefficient of localisation will approach 1·0.

Florence (1962) calculated coefficients of localisation for 140 employment categories in 1930 or 1935 and 1951, using the standard regions of the United Kingdom as the geographical framework. Of the 140 categories, a temporal comparison was not possible in some cases and in others there was no change in the coefficient of localisation; together, these amounted to forty-eight

25

industries. Of the remaining ninety-two industries, fifty-eight showed a decline in the value of the coefficient and thirty-four an increase. Though hardly cast-iron evidence, this does indicate that the tendency toward a wider geographical dispersal of employment categories has been more common than the opposite trend, thus confirming the evidence advanced by other workers.

In 1948, Leser took up the ideas of Florence and developed his own measure of the extent to which a region has a specialised employment structure. The national distribution is taken as the norm, each employment category being expressed as a percentage of the total. Similar percentages are calculated for the region being considered. The national and regional percentages are then compared, to find how much of the region's employment is in common with the national. Leser's coefficient of specialisation amounts to summing the positive differences, to obtain a measure of specialisation that ranges from zero to approaching 100. The former represents no specialisation with respect to the national norm; the latter, full specialisation. This technique is directly analogous to the method some workers have used in urban economic base studies to define the 'export' oriented employment (Isard, et al, 1960).

Using employment data for 1939 and 1947, Leser found that at three levels of employment disaggregation there had been a marked trend toward greater diversification in all regions. His three levels of employment aggregation were:

1.  Three classes covering Primary production, Manufacturing and Services.
2.  Fifteen classes within the Manufacturing sector.
3.  Twenty-five classes comprehending all employment.

Diversification was evident in all three cases. In general, diversification was most evident in those standard regions where specialisation was most marked in 1939; Wales stood out as the region of most striking change.

Conkling (1964) examined the question of diversification in South Wales in a rather different way. He devised an index of diversification analogous to that used by Tress. Dividing the entire labour-force among twenty-three employment classes, he ranked the industries by their percentage share of the total, in ascending order from low to high. If the percentage values are cumulated,

26

they can be plotted as a curve concave upward and lying below the diagonal straight line that represents the situation in which each industry is of equal importance. Taking the area under the curve as a percentage of the area of the triangle bounded by the diagonal, an index is obtained that can range from near zero to near 100. The former extreme represents the concentration of employment in one industry; the latter indicates a uniform distribution among all the categories. (See Chapter 2.) For both South Wales and for Great Britain, Conkling found there was a substantial increase in diversification between 1931 and 1949, though proportionately the change was much greater in South Wales than for the country as a whole. Between 1949 and 1959, the situation was fairly stable, but with a slow decline in diversification at the national level and a somewhat hesitant increase in South Wales.

On the other side of the Bristol Channel, Britton (1967) found evidence of the reverse trend, i.e. a tendency to greater specialisation in the period 1952 to 1962. Of the fourteen sub-regions that he used for his analysis of the Bristol area, only three experienced greater diversification; all of the others tended to specialise. Britton's analysis referred to twenty-nine employment categories covering manufacturing employment and was based on an index of specialisation subsequently used by Keeble and Hauser (see p.19). His study area extended from Gloucester—Cheltenham to Yeovil.

The most recent study is that of Brown (1972). He used Florence's coefficients of localisation and specialisation and applied these to the Main Order industries in nine regions covering Great Britain. For the period 1953 to 1966, all the standard regions experienced diversification of their employment structures, with the biggest changes occurring in those regions of most specialised employment. At the industry level, the general tendency was for greater dispersal: this was true of the manufacturing industries but much more marked for the service employments.

In addition to the works already noted, for which the authors devised and/or used formal tests of trends in the diversification or specialisation of areas, numerous workers have commented on changes in particular regions in a rather less formal manner. By way of example, the north west of England has been especially well documented by D. M. Smith (1969) and also by Cunningham

(1970). From both these works, the impression gained is of diversification of employment in the post-war period, which can of course be ascribed in part to the effects of government regional policy. Much the same appears to be true of Northern Ireland, where the government has made especially strenuous attempts to diversify the province's economy (Steed and Thomas, 1971). The impression from these and other studies reinforces the majority evidence from the formal statistical measures, that diversification has been characteristic of most parts of Britain in recent decades.

### Conclusion

*A priori*, it is to be expected that government attempts to steer development into the depressed regions should have resulted in considerable diversification of local employment structures. This expectation is given credence by the fact that manufacturing industry moving into the peripheral regions differs markedly in structure from the stock of employment previously located there, whereas the reverse is true of industrial employment going to the central regions. And then several empirical studies, addressed to the question of changes in employment specialisation, give clear evidence that diversification has been much more common than increase in specialisation. According to Conkling, most of the change had taken place by 1949, a proposition that is at least consistent with the other evidence cited. Another point to note is the disparate bases of analysis used—disparate geographical areas, time periods, employment disaggregation and techniques. There has not been a complete national study of trends in specialisation/ diversification. Indeed, in his review of the economic literature, Brown (1969) did not even mention the topic of diversification directly, though giving some attention to shift-and-share studies designed to disaggregate regional growth into components reflecting the structure of employment and regionally differentiated rates of growth in the individual employment categories. However, it must be noted that in a more recent study (1972), Brown did give some attention to the question of specialisation/diversification.

In the absence of a thorough national study, comparable in scope to the analyses of the United States by Rodgers (1955) and Fuchs (1962), the present study has been undertaken to fill part of the gap. Particular emphasis is laid on patterns of diversification/specialisation, though attention is also given to the changing localisation of individual industries. For reasons that are discussed in the next chapter, the period of study covers 1959 to 1968, the geographical framework is the sixty-one economic planning sub-regions and employment is disaggregated to the 152 industries identified as the Minimum List Headings (MLH).

# Chapter 2  Concepts and Data

In the previous chapter, brief mention was made of several techniques by which the degree of employment diversification in an area can be measured. No attempt was made there to discuss the advantages and disadvantages of the various methods, or to consider other approaches that might be adopted. Clearly, though, it is essential to define the concepts of diversification and its opposite, specialisation, and to find an operationally convenient way of expressing the concepts so defined.

The characteristic feature of Florence's approach is his use of the national distribution of employment as the bench-mark against which to compare the distribution of a particular industry. In devising his coefficient of localisation, Florence was specifically interested in the distribution of particular industries among regions within the country. However, his ideas may be translated into terms specifically relevant to the consideration of areal specialisation in the following way. Table 2.1 shows some hypothetical data for Great Britain and for an imaginary area within the nation. At the national level, employment is shown as fairly uniformly spread among the five industry classes, whereas in imaginary area A industry 4 dominates the labour market. Subtracting the national percentages from those for area A gives the differences shown in the right-hand column; algebraically, these sum to zero. The positive deviations add to 20. If we follow Florence's practice (his coefficient of localisation) and use the positive deviations and divide by 100, a coefficient is obtained of 0·2. If area A had a distribution of employment identical to the national pattern, the coefficient would be zero. At the other extreme, were area A to have only one kind of employment, the coefficient would approach 1·0.

Such a coefficient of specialisation, analogous to Florence's coefficient of localisation, measures the extent to which the distribution of employment in an area diverges from the national distribution. If one wishes to examine changes that are going on over time, a fundamental problem immediately obtrudes. The national distribution of employment is itself likely to be changing

**Table 2.1**  Hypothetical employment data for Great Britain and for an imaginary area, in per cent.

| Industry | Imaginary area A | Great Britain | Difference + or — |
|---|---|---|---|
| 1 | 5 | 10 | —5 |
| 2 | 25 | 20 | +5 |
| 3 | 10 | 20 | —10 |
| 4 | 40 | 25 | +15 |
| 5 | 20 | 25 | —5 |
| Total | 100 | 100 | |

and therefore the 'bench-mark' on which comparison is based is not a constant. To interpret changes in the regions relative to the national norm, it is necessary also to examine the behaviour of the national pattern as, for example, Chisholm (1968, pp.83–5) did in an analysis of the localisation of horticultural crops.

The approaches adopted by Tress and Conkling get over this difficulty. To visualise the underlying concept, refer to Figure 2.1. Given N industries, rank them according to the percentage employment and obtain the cumulated percentage. If employment is uniformly distributed among the industry categories, the resulting curve will be as 'a' in the figure. To the extent that employment is concentrated in some categories, the curve will diverge from this norm, as 'b' and 'c'. Note that in Figure 2.1, the industries have been ranked from largest to smallest, so that curves 'b' and 'c' lie above 'a': Conkling adopted the opposite procedure. The extent to which curves 'b' and 'c' diverge from 'a' can be expressed in either of two ways. Conkling calculated the area under (over) the curve ('b' or 'c') as a proportion of the area of the right-angled triangle formed by curve 'a'. An alternative, adopted by Tress, is illustrated by the hypothetical data in Table 2.2, that can be thought of as representing three regions comparable to curves 'a', 'b' and 'c' in Figure 2.1. The left-hand part of the table shows the percentage distribution of employment among five industries, whereas in the right the percentages are accumulated. In the case illustrated, the ranking from largest industry to smallest does not involve re-ordering the industries. If we take area 'a', with a uniform distribution of employment, the sum of the cumulated percentages is 300. At the other extreme, the sum for 'c' is 500.

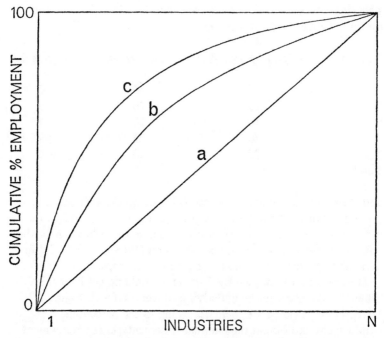

Fig. 2.1 Representation of the Lorenz curve mode of analysis.

The fundamental property of these two variants of Lorenz curve analysis (Conkling and Tress) is that changes over time for any one area are compared with a constant value (a uniform distribution among the industry classes) instead of with a shifting norm (the national distribution of employment). This same property is also a feature of the index of specialisation used by

**Table 2.2** Derivation of the Tress statistic.

| Industry | Percentage employment | | | Cumulated % employment | | |
|---|---|---|---|---|---|---|
| | a | b | c | a | b | c |
| 1 | 20 | 50 | 100 | 20 | 50 | 100 |
| 2 | 20 | 25 | 0 | 40 | 75 | 100 |
| 3 | 20 | 10 | 0 | 60 | 85 | 100 |
| 4 | 20 | 10 | 0 | 80 | 95 | 100 |
| 5 | 20 | 5 | 0 | 100 | 100 | 100 |
| Total | 100 | 100 | 100 | 300 | 405 | 500 |

Britton and subsequently Keeble and Hauser. It will be recollected (p.19) that this index takes the form:

$$I = \sqrt{P^2_1 + P^2_2 + \ldots\ldots P^2_n}$$

If, for example, there were 100 industry classes then a uniform distribution of employment would yield an index of 1·0. On the other hand, were all employment to be concentrated in one industry, the index would be 100. Thus, the maximum value of the index is invariably 100 but the lower limit varies according to the number of industry classes.

However, neither the Tress statistic nor the Conkling version of Lorenz curve analysis nor Britton's index of specialisation permit one to state whether any change in the level of diversification in an area between two time periods is statistically significant. If we consider only one geographical area at two points in time (1959 and 1968 in the present study), we have two areas of employment by industry classes (which number 152 in the present case). It is clear that the distribution in 1968 is at least partly conditioned by the situation in 1959; probably to a very large extent in fact. As the two data sets are not independent of each other, the chi-squared test is not appropriate as a means for determining whether a significant change in industrial structure has occurred. On the other hand, the Wilcoxon matched-pairs signed-ranks test (Siegel, 1956) is designed for just this situation.

The principle of the Wilcoxon test is to obtain the differences in absolute employment for each industry class, to rank these differences irrespective of sign and then to ask whether or not the pluses or minuses (whichever yields the lesser sum) are randomly distributed over the range of the differences. A distribution which is not significantly different from random implies no structural change, whereas a non-random spread indicates that there is a change in structure that cannot be attributed to chance.

Given that employment data are subject to secular growth or decline, it is essential as a first step to standardise the data to eliminate temporal trend effects. For this purpose, the employment total for each area in 1959 has been adjusted to the 1968 level by means of an equal proportionate change for each industry class, rounded to the nearest whole number. With the data thus standardised, the Wilcoxon test provides a tool for establishing whether significant structural changes have occurred over time; it is not, however, suitable for comparing the structure of two different areas at the same time. Though the Wilcoxon statistic incorporates a measure for the direction of change, this direction of change refers to whether the positive or negative values predominate in the industry classes with a high (low) rank by absolute change. Nothing can be inferred from this as to whether the region has become more or less diversified.

In principle, therefore, a two-stage operation may be envisaged. The first is to apply the Wilcoxon statistic to all areas to ascertain which have experienced a significant change in structure. In all cases where no significant change is recorded, it might be assumed that only random events have occurred. In all other cases, some systematic processes may be presumed to be operative and the nature of these can be probed by versions of the Lorenz curve, though levels of significance cannot be attached thereto.

Consideration was given to two other approaches to the measurement of diversification or specialisation of employment in regions, but both were rejected. The first to note is the concentration ratio. This ratio expresses the proportion of the total employment in an area that is accounted for by a specified number of the largest industries. Fuchs (1962) used the percentage of employment in the single largest industry, whereas Evely and Little (1960) and Bain (1966) preferred to use the three or four main industries. The main defect of this approach is the large amount of information that may be suppressed. As a technique it is probably best suited to the study of monopoly, for which purpose it has been quite widely used; but for this purpose, concentration ratios express the proportion of an industry's output that originates from one or a limited number of firms, not the proportion of an area's employment attributable to a particular industry (or industries). In the context of the present study, concentration ratios lose too much information to be an acceptable technique.

Recently, there has been introduced a new version of the Lorenz curve idea under the name of entropy (Theil, 1967; Horowitz, 1970). Entropy (H) for a region is defined as:

$$H = -\Sigma [q_i \log_2 (q_i)]$$

where $q_i$ is the employment share of the nth industry in region q. This equation is equivalent to:

$$H = -\Sigma \left[ \frac{q_i \; \log_{10} \; (q_i)}{\log_{10}(2)} \right]$$

Employment share is written as a decimal proportion of 1·0, i.e. 0·1 is equivalent to 10 per cent. If we imagine any region with N industries, entropy is obtained as the sum of the products of employment share and the logarithm thereof divided by the constant 0·301 (the logarithm of 2 to the base 10). The result is a numerical scale that ranges from zero when all the employment is concentrated in one industry to an upper limit that varies with N, the number of industry classes used. In all cases, H is a positive value, since the negative sign on the right of the equation cancels out the fact that the logarithm of a decimal number is itself negative.

No formal test of significance is available whereby different entropy values may be compared. In this respect, therefore, the Tress statistic and the entropy approach are entirely equivalent. They differ, however, in two important respects. The entropy approach has a great advantage where comparison is to be made between situations in which the number of classes varies. That is, a doubling of the number of classes raises the maximum feasible score by 1·00. For example, a uniform distribution of employment among five industry classes yields an H value of 2·32 whereas a similar distribution among ten classes yields a statistic of 3·32. The Tress statistic does not possess this characteristic nor one that is similar. The second difference is that the Tress statistic involves the ranking of the industry classes from largest to smallest, which takes a good deal of computer time. Derivation of the H values from the entropy approach does not require this iterative search and therefore is less demanding of computing time.

The first of these differences is not relevant for the present study, since in any one operation the number of industry classes is constant. The second difference—the relative computational economy of the entropy statistic—might have led to its selection in preference to the Tress statistic, had all else been equal. The inequality of conditions, however, lay in the fact that work had already progressed quite far on the basis of the Tress statistic before the possibilities of the entropy approach were realised. At that point in time, a switch to the entropy statistic and the consequential need to recalculate data would have entailed additional computer time of the same order as was required by continuing with the Tress statistic, plus the time for preparing and testing the relevant programme.

However, the main issue is whether use of one statistic would yield results at variance with the conclusions derived by the use of another measure of industrial specialisation. A comparatively simple test was carried out by Diana Kershaw (1971). Using the same sixty-one sub-regions used in the present study and total employment for the years 1959 and 1968 but disaggregated only to the twenty-four SIC orders instead of the 152 MLH categories, she calculated the Tress and entropy scores for both years. A simple linear correlation of the two scores yielded $r^2$ values of 0·931 and 0·972 for the respective years. It seems reasonable to conclude that the two approaches yield essentially the same results and that it is therefore immaterial which is used. Further work along the same lines has been undertaken by Forer and Ferguson (1973), using the MLH data and a larger number of indices of concentration. Their results confirm those obtained by Kershaw.

Hart's 1971 paper is also worth noting. Though his analysis was framed with reference to the traditional concern of economists with the extent of concentration within industries (i.e. with questions of monopoly and competition) the major conclusion to which he came is relevant in the present context. He concluded that where the number of observations is large, the entropy approach is inferior to 'traditional' measures of business concentration, and that the same conclusion holds for small numbers as well. In the case of large numbers, Hart preferred to use the variance in the data; in the second case, of small numbers, he concluded that cumulative concentration curves should be used. In the present study, we are dealing with large numbers and as measures of variance are not particularly appropriate for the task in hand, it seems clear that some version of Lorenz curve analysis is to be preferred—which is what the Tress statistic is.

In reviewing the statistical techniques that might be used for measuring changes in the degree of regional specialisation of employment, we examined Isard *et al* (1960) and other sources

(e.g. Hoover, 1971). This search did not reveal any approaches
additional to those discussed above or referred to in Chapter 1.
Thus, for the purpose of examining changes in the degree of local
specialisation/diversification, the statistical methods used have
been two; the Tress statistic to measure the magnitude and
direction of change and the Wilcoxon matched-pairs signed-ranks
test to establish whether changes can be regarded as significant.

Now, attention has been focused on the structure of employment
in regions and changes thereof over time. In other words, in
Figure 2.2 we have been considering exclusively the *rows* of the
employment matrix. It is immediately evident that precisely the
same concepts of specialisation/diversification apply to the *columns*,
i.e. to the individual industries, only the names given to the
dichotomous extremes are localisation and dispersal of industry.
For both the Wilcoxon and Tress statistics, precisely the same
computer programmes can be applied with equal facility to the
rows and the columns of the matrix. The only difference in using
the Wilcoxon test lies in the standardisation of the data to

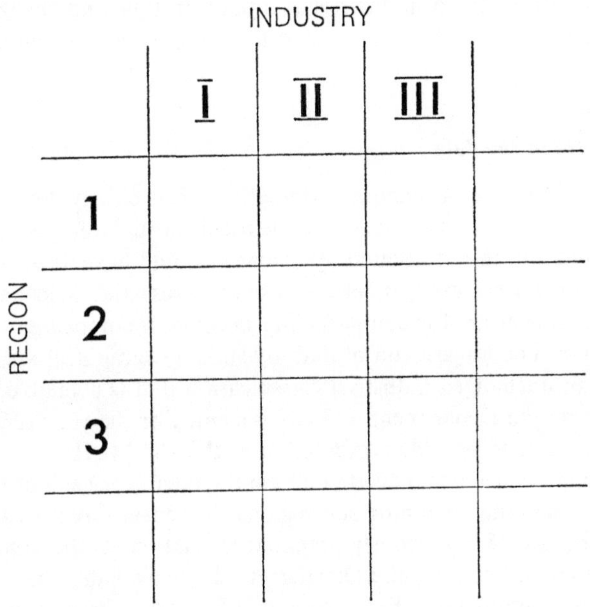

Fig. 2.2   Representation of a three-region three-industry matrix.

eliminate secular change. Thus, in applying the test to changes in the structure of employment in an area, the 1959 employment for the *area* is adjusted to the 1968 total; whereas to test for changes in the localisation of an industry, it is the *industry* total which must be adjusted (see p.33).

The combination of the Wilcoxon and Tress statistics allows a sensitive analysis of changes in structure to be undertaken and together they provide the main statistical techniques that have been employed in this study. There is, however, one kind of problem for which these techniques are not appropriate and for which another approach must be adopted. If we ask the question: how similar is the structure of employment in one region to the structure in another? then at least at the descriptive level, standard correlation yielding values for $r^2$ is probably the most acceptable technique. In this way, areas can be identified that are more similar to the national structure than are other areas; similarly, those areas which are more nearly similar to each other can be identified. Such comparisons can be made for 1959 and 1968 and also for the pattern of change over that time period. By the same token, the spatial distributions of industries at a point in time and changes over time, can be compared. But no tests of significance can be applied.

### The nature of the data

For the purpose of temporal comparison, it is clearly desirable that the industrial classification be identical throughout the period considered and that no boundary changes should have affected the geographical areas used. Indeed, to use the Tress and Wilcoxon statistics, this desire for comparability becomes a compelling imperative. The longest run of data by small geographical areas and on an unchanged industrial classification that is available was supplied by the Department of Employment. For the year 1968, they were able to provide a tabulation of the 152 MLH employment categories, covering all employment, for each of the sixty-one economic planning sub-regions that cover Great Britain. In the absence of a previously prepared tabulation on the same basis for an earlier year, the Department made available the records for Employment Exchanges in 1959. From these records, it was possible to compile totals for the sixty-one sub-regions. In so doing, a number of adjustments must be made to overcome two difficulties. The first arises from the fact that in a few cases the 1959 Employment Exchange areas cross the boundaries of the 1968 sub-regions. In the second place, for some of the Exchanges some of the MLH categories were amalgamated to prevent disclosure of employment on work of strategic importance. The number of adjustments in both categories and their individual size were not likely to introduce serious errors into the sub-regional totals. In any case, every endeavour was made to reduce the errors of estimation; for example, in allocating parts of an Exchange area to two or more sub-regions, data on total populations at the parish level are readily available and can be used as the basis for assigning employment, while employment totals at the standard region level provide a bench-mark to which to work.

The data were made available to us for both male and female employment. For the work reported in the present book, we have used the sum of both male and female workers, i.e. the total workforce. As for the choice of the years 1959 and 1968, these represent the terminal years for the longest run of statistics using the same industrial classification. Though notionally data for 1958 are available on the same basis, they are regarded as unreliable because 1958 was the first year for operating a new classification. By 1959 the initial errors and confusions had been ironed out. 1968, on the other hand, is the last year before another reclassification was introduced. We have not used data for the intervening years, because of the trouble its provision would have caused the Department of Employment and the gargantuan problems of data handling with which we would have been faced.

However, the two years are in fact remarkably suitable for the purpose in hand. As Figure 2.3 shows, Gross Domestic Product was growing steadily, though not dramatically, in both the periods centred on 1959 and 1968, and in both cases the growth rate then current represented an acceleration over the immediately preceding period. 1959 was a year of peak unemployment, with a mean total of 475,000 out of work; 1968 was also a peak year (564,000 unemployed), but the peak is almost imperceptible and really represents a stand-still in the dreary climb to one million unemployed at the end of 1971 and early 1972. (However, if Gujarati's interpretation is correct, a structural change occurred about 1966 in the relationship between unemployment and the level of economic activity. On his adjusted unemployment series, 1967 was a year of peak unemployment at a level somewhat below the 1959 level and with a marked decline through 1968 and 1969. See Gujarati, 1972.) In terms of unfilled vacancies, 1959 and 1968 were both years in which the total stood a little above the minimum point reached the previous year, the totals being respectively 224,000 and 271,000. Thus, the two years represent roughly comparable points on the cyclical pattern of economic activity, with totals of unemployment and of vacant jobs at much the same level. Consequently, we may reasonably assume that attempts to measure secular changes in aspects of the economy will not be seriously vitiated by cyclical variations in business activity.

Furthermore, the period straddles the change from complacency about regional problems evident in the Local Employment Act of 1860, which abolished the Development Areas and replaced them by Development Districts, to much greater concern and much increased government intervention, which occurred especially with the advent of a Labour administration in 1964. Almost certainly the increase in government intervention during the period could not have had a dramatic effect on regional employment structure within four years, so that any changes which can be detected may

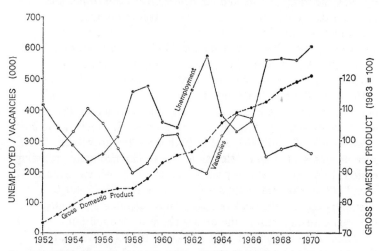

Fig. 2.3   United Kingdom: trends in Gross National Product, unemployment and vacancies.

fairly be ascribed to the combination of long-term trends and a
moderate level of government intervention.

## Operational procedures

There is no need to discuss the operational procedures in detail,
as they are for the most part entirely straightforward. The first
task was to obtain the 1959 data in a format comparable with the
1968 set, to provide two matrices 61 $\times$ 152, i.e., 61 sub-regions and
152 MLH classes. For most of the operations, it was the
manipulation of these raw employment totals that was undertaken.
However, as pointed out already (p.38), to use the Wilcoxon test
for significant changes in employment structure, it is necessary to
eliminate the effects of secular change. For this purpose, therefore,
two further matrices had to be prepared, in each case adjusting the
1959 matrix to the relevant totals for 1968. In terms of Figure 2.2,
to test for changes in the structure of employment in a sub-region
means adjusting the rows of the 1959 matrix by a uniform
proportion so that the sum is equal to the 1968 sum for the row.
However, to perform the Wilcoxon test for changes in the
localisation of an industry, it is the columns that are so adjusted.
The summation of the row and column totals is of course the
same in both cases, but the distribution of values within the
respective adjusted matrices differs somewhat.

At this stage, there is no need to discuss procedures further.
At relevant points in the ensuing text, details will be dealt with as
appropriate.

# Chapter 3    Sub-Regional Changes in Employment Structure

By way of introducing this chapter, it is useful to refer to
Figure 3.1, showing the quintile groupings of sub-regions according
to the percentage change in total employment over the period
1959 to 1968. This shows very clearly that practically all the
sub-regions with marked growth lie south of the line from the
Wash to the Dee. Within this southern zone, the conurbations of
Birmingham and London stand out, the latter having experienced
a substantial fall in total employment. North of the Wash–Dee
line, the only area with substantial growth lies on the south side
of the Humber, sub-region 7 which includes Scunthorpe and
Grimsby. With a mean growth of 6.1 per cent for all sub-regions
and a range from −11 to +32 per cent, there has clearly been
considerable scope for structural adjustment to occur despite the
relatively short period of time covered.

**The Wilcoxon test**

The first exercise was to see whether the matched-pairs signed-
rank test identified parts of the country in which significant changes
in the structure of employment have occurred. For this purpose, all
152 classes of the MLH list have been used. Figure 3.2 shows that
in fact only eight sub-regions experienced a sufficient change in
structure to be regarded as significant at levels of 99 per cent or
higher using a one-tailed test. These eight are scattered from north
to south of the country, represent fast and slow growing (even
declining) sub-regions and include both rural and urban areas.
Altogether, a discouragingly fragmented pattern providing few
clues as to the likely explanatory factors. Even when the confidence
level is lowered to 95 per cent, the only substantial tract of country
that is identified runs from Norfolk, north of Birmingham and
along the Welsh Marches. Altogether, only sixteen sub-regions
showed a change significant at the 95 per cent level or over, or
approximately one-quarter of the sub-regions. For the rest of the
country, change was not dramatic enough to be accepted as
statistically significant.

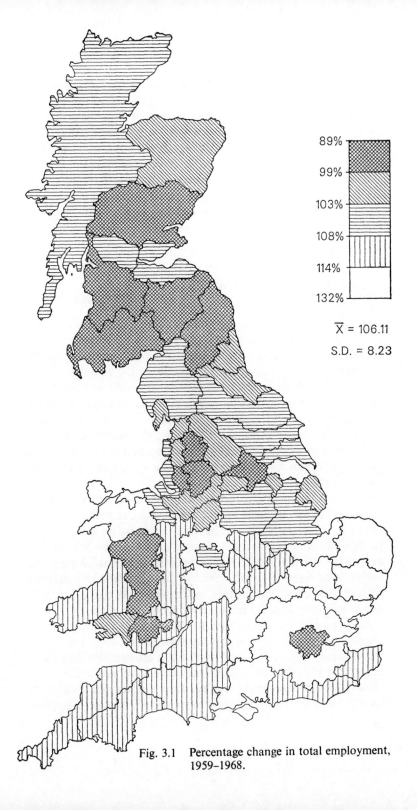

89%
99%
103%
108%
114%
132%

$\overline{X}$ = 106.11
S.D. = 8.23

Fig. 3.1  Percentage change in total employment,
1959–1968.

If the question of significance is ignored for the moment, the Wilcoxon test statistic, or $Z$ value, may be treated as the dependent variable and correlated with other, independent, variables. For this purpose, the sub-regions were grouped into two: one group with a percentage growth above the national mean of 6·1 per cent and the other below (including actual decline in total employment). There is no *a priori* reason to suppose that the two groups will behave differently, since both rapid growth and rapid decline may be concentrated upon a limited number of industries or be spread widely. Nevertheless, the results as set out below are interesting:

sub-regions with above-average growth
$$Z = 7·543 - 0·056X \qquad r^2 = 0·174 \qquad F = 5·259$$
sub-regions with below-average growth (or decline)
$$Z = 12·992 - 0·117X \qquad r^2 = 0·230 \qquad F = 8·383$$

where X is the employment in 1968 as a percentage of the 1959 total. The former relationship is significant at the 95 per cent level and the latter at the 99 per cent level. The first equation indicates that the greater the rate of growth, the lower the value for $Z$, implying that rapid growth is associated with little structural change. On the other hand, a low or negative growth rate implies smaller values for X the greater the decline in employment and hence an increasing value of $Z$. We may infer, therefore, that a fall (or low rate of growth) in total employment is associated with greater structural changes than occurs in sub-regions experiencing rapid growth.

Although the statistical significance of these results is clearly open to question, perhaps the important point to note is the *direction* of the relationship. The faster a sub-region has grown, the less has been its structural change; the slower the growth, the greater the structural shift. If slow growth were equated with regions receiving special aid, then this finding would be consistent with the hypothesis put forward in Chapter 1. As this condition is not met (Figure 3.1), the matter is evidently complicated.

These initial experiments with the Wilcoxon test were discouraging and suggested that attempts to find academic respectability in high levels of significance are vain. Perhaps the main reason for this initially disappointing result lies in the relatively short time period studied, given the inherent stability of the economic system over considerable periods of time. Therefore,

44

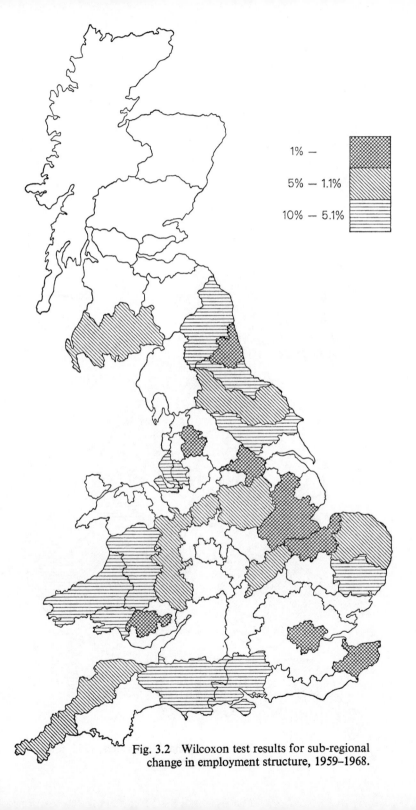

Fig. 3.2   Wilcoxon test results for sub-regional
change in employment structure, 1959–1968.

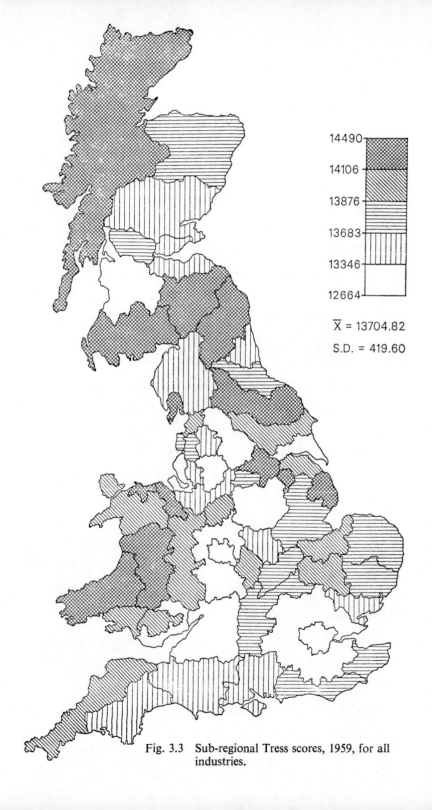

14490
14106
13876
13683
13346
12664

$\overline{X}$ = 13704.82
S.D. = 419.60

Fig. 3.3   Sub-regional Tress scores, 1959, for all
          industries.

further work was not undertaken on sub-regional structural changes using the Wilcoxon test—for example, by differentiating manufacturing and service industries—and we resigned ourselves to placing main reliance on the descriptive Tress statistic. However, this statistic has one great advantage over the Wilcoxon test—it shows the direction of change, toward or away from diversification.

## Tress Statistic

Initially, it is convenient to describe the results of calculating the Tress scores for the sixty-one sub-regions and then to proceed to a discussion of the patterns that are revealed and the reasons that may explain them. In this discussion, it should be remembered that with 152 industry classes, the Tress statistic has a range from 7,650 to 15,200. The former figure represents complete diversification, in the sense of a uniform distribution of employment among all categories; the latter arises if all employment is concentrated in one industry.

Figures 3.3 and 3.4 show the degree of diversification in both 1959 and 1968, taking account of all 152 industry classes. Perhaps the most striking feature of Figure 3.3 is that, apart from the London area, central Scotland and a couple of other sub-regions (centred respectively on Newcastle-upon-Tyne and Hull), the areas that are relatively diversified form a more-or-less continuous belt of country from Cumberland to Dorset. Both to the west, in Wales, and along the eastern part of the country, including parts of Yorkshire, the local economies are more highly specialised. By 1968, the position in Scotland had deteriorated somewhat, as also in the south west. Elsewhere, the pattern in 1968 is essentially the same as in 1959, except for some hint that the belt of high diversification had filled out and become somewhat more aligned along the London-Merseyside axis.

Main interest, however, attaches to changes over time in the Tress scores. Between 1959 and 1968, the mean Tress score for the sixty-one sub-regions declined slightly, from 13,705 to 13,610. At the same time, the standard deviation dropped more sharply, from 420 to 371. Thus, over the period there was a small and possibly not significant trend to diversification, accompanied by a strong tendency for the structure in the sub-regions to converge toward the national average. This implies both that the highly specialised

47

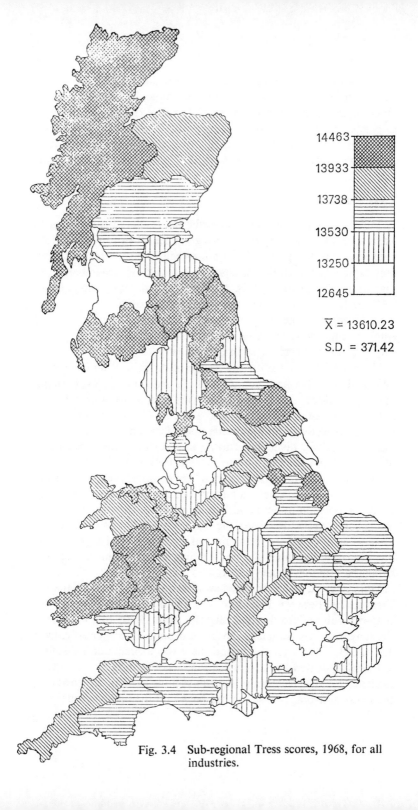

14463
13933
13738
13530
13250
12645

$\overline{X}$ = 13610.23
S.D. = 371.42

Fig. 3.4  Sub-regional Tress scores, 1968, for all industries.

sub-regions diversified, and the well diversified ones tended to become more specialised. Consequently, there ought to be manifest strongly marked geographical differences in the Tress statistic changes.

Figure 3.5 shows that indeed there are marked differences in the behaviour of the sub-regions. Note that in compiling this map, the Tress score for 1968 has been subtracted from the 1959 value. The effect is that a positive difference means there has been diversification over the period, and a negative difference indicates a tendency toward greater specialisation. Roughly south of the line between the Humber and Cardigan Bay, the pattern of change is remarkably clear-cut. In the central zone running from Birmingham to London, there has either been an increase in specialisation or only a weak increase in diversification, whereas the peripheral sub-regions have experienced a strongly marked shift toward diversification. In the northern part of England and in Scotland, the pattern is rather more complex, though the tendency toward diversification along the east coast is quite marked.

For the country as a whole, twelve sub-regions fall into the quintile group with a change in Tress score in the range of $+3$ to $-369$; all other sub-regions experienced at least a modest diversification of their employment structure.

A point of some interest is that the arc of country which was identified by the Wilcoxon test as experiencing significant structural change in employment, running from Herefordshire north of Birmingham and across to East Anglia, has in fact been diversifying. There is some suggestion here that where a statistically significant change in employment structure has occurred, it has primarily been in the direction of diversification rather than specialisation, but the hint is a slender one that cannot be taken too seriously.

The overall picture can conveniently be disaggregated to distinguish between manufacturing industries (MLH 211 to 499 inclusive) and the service industries (MLH numbers 500 to 906). The former group comprises 108 industry classes, while the latter numbers thirty-seven. The primary industries (agriculture, forestry, fishing, mining and quarrying) are covered by only seven MLH categories and it hardly seems warranted to calculate Tress scores for such a small number of industries.

Discussion of the static patterns as of 1959 and 1968 for the

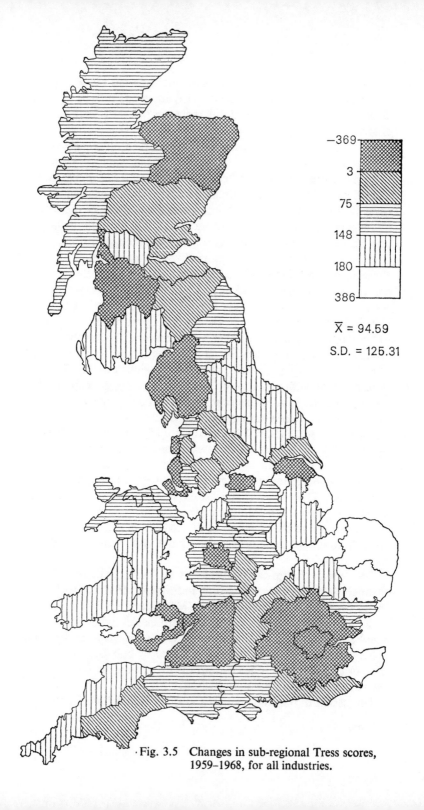

$\overline{X}$ = 94.59
S.D. = 125.31

Fig. 3.5   Changes in sub-regional Tress scores,
1959–1968, for all industries.

two industry classes does not add significantly to the picture that has already been described. However, the changes over time are revealing. For manufacturing industries alone, numbering 108 altogether, the theoretical range of the Tress statistic is from 5,450 to 10,800, i.e. considerably lower figures than for 152 industries. Yet, as Figure 3.6 shows, the range in the absolute change in scores is greater than for all employment. There is a broad similarity in the patterns shown in Figures 3.5 and 3.6, but with manufacturing industries alone there has been a somewhat greater tendency for Wales, the south-west and the industrial north to diversity. It is also noteworthy that Scotland has fared somewhat better relative to the country as a whole. It is when we turn to Figure 3.7 that a startling difference emerges. With only thirty-seven classes at the MLH level, the Tress statistic ranges from 1,900 to 3,700. For the country as a whole, the predominant change has been for sub-regions to become more highly specialised, a tendency opposite to that for manufacturing alone and for all employment. Furthermore, the geographical pattern is most curious. Three areas of increasing diversity in service employment stand out; much of the South East except London itself; the Severnside-South Wales area; and the east coast from the Wash to south of Teesside. Apart from north-west Scotland, which has a very small total employment, diversification of service employment is elsewhere found in isolated pockets in north-west England and north Wales. Scotland and central Wales stand out as regions of substantial extent experiencing a marked increase in the degree of specialisation of service employment.

This brief discussion of Figures 3.3 to 3.7 shows quite clearly that there are marked spatial variations in the direction and extent of change, toward or away from diversification. Clearly the spatial patterns are complex and it is therefore of interest to enquire whether the initial hypotheses postulated in Chapter 1 can be verified or not. Consequently, we will turn to the task of trying to explain the patterns that have been observed.

## Employment and the size of the local economy

*A priori* reasoning suggests that the larger the total employment in a sub-region, the more diverse the structure of employment is likely to be. To test for this possibility, the Tress score (152

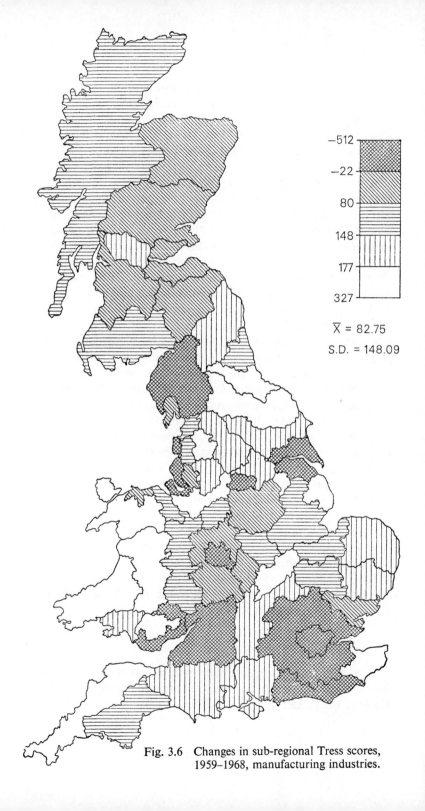

Fig. 3.6 Changes in sub-regional Tress scores, 1959–1968, manufacturing industries.

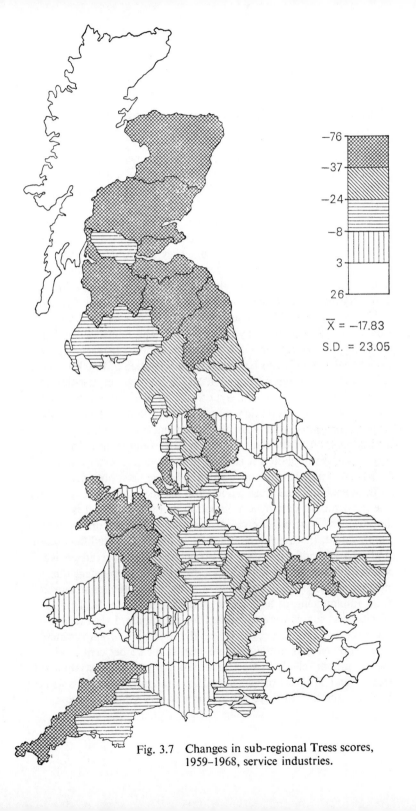

Fig. 3.7 Changes in sub-regional Tress scores,
1959–1968, service industries.

industry classes) for each sub-region was regressed on the total employment, for 1959 and 1968, with the following results:

$$1968 \quad Y = 17,145 - 669 \cdot 5 \log X \quad r^2 = 0 \cdot 690 \quad F = 127 \cdot 345$$
$$1959 \quad Y = 17,864 - 791 \cdot 2 \log X \quad r^2 = 0 \cdot 748 \quad F = 175 \cdot 218$$

where Y is the Tress score and X the employment for the sub-region. These highly significant results show quite clearly that diversity of employment is associated with the absolute size of the workforce and in the manner that is to be expected.

This very high level of explanation, while intuitively plausible, appears to conflict with results reported by Clemente and Sturgis (1971) for the United States. Though they obtained a positive association between community size and degree of diversification, the over-all value of $r^2$ was only $0 \cdot 168$; among the four regions covering the country, the value for $r^2$ ranged from a low figure of $0 \cdot 129$ to a high of $0 \cdot 303$. They used an index of specialisation similar to that employed by Britton (1967) and related this to the resident population, for 535 urban areas sampled from the 1,899 which in the 1960 census had a resident population of 10,000 or more. Clemente and Sturgis commented on the low level of association achieved and offered several hypotheses by which the result could be explained. However, they apparently overlooked the possibility that the relationship may be non-linear and undertook no transformation of the data. Had they, for example, used the logarithm of population it is quite possible that a result more nearly comparable with our own would have been obtained.

In interpreting the close association between the Tress score and the logarithm of employed population in a sub-region, it is important to note the skewed distribution of sub-regions by total employment, there being comparatively few that exceed 0·5 million and a bare handful in excess of 1·0 million. Therefore, it seemed worthwhile carrying out two other exercises to supplement the normalisation procedure embodied in the use of the logarithm of total employment, in both cases using the 1968 date. In the first place, Tress scores were calculated for the standard regions and these scores were then regressed on the logarithm of employment. The relationship is not acceptable even at the 95 per cent level. Next, random selections were made from among the sixty-one sub-regions and Tress scores calculated for the synthetic regions formed by amalgamation of these sub-regions. Ninety synthetic regions

54

were formed, comprising ten pairs, ten trios, etc., up to ten regions comprising ten sub-regions. In the selection process, no contiguity constraint was imposed but for each trial a sub-region that had already been included in that trial could not be selected a second time. The effect of this procedure is to generate a selection of regions with a larger proportion that have a sizeable labour force than is the case with the sixty-one original sub-regions. The result obtained is:

$$Y_1 = 15{,}767 - 458 \cdot 6 \log X_1 \quad r^2 = 0 \cdot 470 \quad F = 76 \cdot 352$$

where $Y_1$ is the Tress score and $X_1$ the total employment of the synthetic regions.

It is notable that the correlation is lower for the synthetic regions than for the sixty-one sub-regions. Figure 3·8 indicates why this may be so. Most of the synthetic regions exceed 1·0 million employees and in this sector of the diagram there appears to be relatively little systematic variation in the degree of employment diversification with the size of the total workforce. Indeed, although formal comparison of the slopes of the three regressions shown is not valid because the equations are not independent of each other, there is a strong hint that as the level of aggregation increases so does the slope of the regression flatten. It is evident that where total employment is less than 1·0 million there is a close association between diversity of employment structure and the total workforce. Above the million mark, this relationship is much weaker, if not entirely absent. We thus have confirmation of a crucial step in Thompson's proposition (see p.20), that small cities (or regions) are likely to have more specialised economies than large ones.

Although the equations reported on p.54 account for a respectable proportion of the variance in sub-regional Tress scores, there may be a systematic distribution of the residuals. To examine this possibility, Tress scores were estimated from the total employment and these estimated values were subtracted from the actual Tress scores. This exercise was undertaken for both 1959 and 1968, using the Tress statistic calculated for all 152 industries. Given that there is a high level of temporal auto-correlation in the data, the spatial patterns for the two years are similar. However, for 1968 the results are somewhat more coherent than for 1959, and are presented in Figure 3.9. The upper quintile values indicate

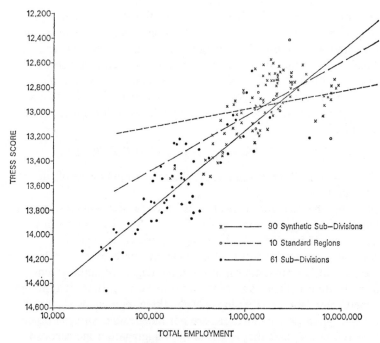

Fig. 3.8  Relationship of 1968 Tress score (all industries) and total
sub-regional employment.

that the actual Tress score is in excess of that which is to be
expected on the basis of employed population, consequently
showing that the local employment structure is more specialised
than would be anticipated. Conversely, the lower quintile values
indicate employment structures that are more diversified than
might be expected.

London and the areas to the south and west stand out as a
continuous block of country with an employment structure more
specialised than would be supposed. This characteristic extends
north-westwards to include the Birmingham conurbation. The
other major area that shares this characteristic runs from south of
the Humber up the east coast into southern Scotland. Two regions
with the opposite characteristic are centred respectively on the
Lancashire industrial areas and south-east Wales: with the adjacent
sub-regions, there is a general tendency for the west coast between
the Severn and Clyde estuaries to have a relatively diversified

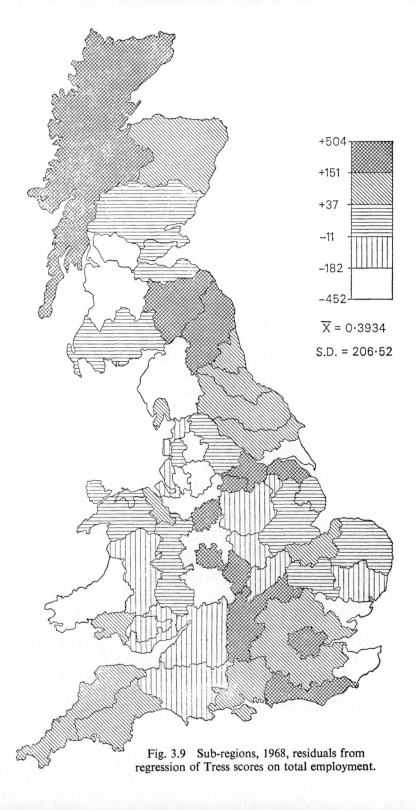

+504
+151
+37
−11
−182
−452

$\overline{X}$ = 0·3934

S.D. = 206·52

Fig. 3.9  Sub-regions, 1968, residuals from
regression of Tress scores on total employment.

structure of employment. However, the overall pattern is not very clear-cut.

Reference has already been made to the fact of temporal autocorrelation in the Tress scores. Simple correlation of the Tress statistics for the two years yields an $r^2$ value of 0·916, while correlation of the residuals from the regression equations shows a lower association, the $r^2$ being 0·716. Although these associations are high, and suggest a permanence in the structural patterns that has been little modified in the time-period of our study, it has already been shown that substantial changes in the spatial patterns have occurred and it is to a further examination of these changes that we now turn.

### Changing degree of specialisation

We have already shown that in both 1959 and 1968 there was a close association between the total employment in a region and the level of diversification. The results shown on p.54 indicate that there has been some decline in the degree of association over the period of our study, $r^2$ having fallen from 0·748 to 0·690. However, for the moment it is more interesting to consider the regression equations. The fact that there has been a secular tendency for factories and other places of employment to become larger in terms of the number of employees (Chisholm, 1970, pp.61–62), on account of internal economies of scale, suggests that with the passage of time a given level of diversification can only be achieved with a larger total workforce. We would therefore expect there to be a sideways shift in the relationship between the Tress score and total employment. On this expectation, we would suppose that the intercept value (a coefficient) in the regression equations would increase between 1959 and 1968, while the slope (b coefficient) would remain constant; such a change would mean that for any given employed total population, the Tress score would be higher in 1968 than in 1959: a high Tress score indicates a specialised structure of employment.

In the event, our expectations are not borne out. Between 1959 and 1968, the intercept value has declined while at the same time the slope of the regression has flattened. These changes in the form of the relationship are consistent with the decline in the level of correlation and indicate that sub-regions with a small total employment have a greater chance of a diversified pattern of employment than formerly was the case. If this trend should be sustained, it does of course have important policy implications, in that one of the putative advantages of large centres (diversified employment) may become less than is normally supposed.

The fact that sub-regions with a small total employment tend to be more specialised in their employment structure than larger ones suggests one mechanism that may account for the spatial variation in the temporal changes in specialisation. We would expect sub-regions with a growing total employment to be diversifying; we would further expect that the greater the increase in total employment, the greater the diversification. The converse proposition could be expected to be true of those sub-regions in decline. Notwithstanding the somewhat inconclusive results from the Wilcoxon $Z$ scores, which pointed to precisely the opposite conclusion (p.44), it is worth examining the Tress scores in the light of this expectation. The change in Tress score (1959 minus 1968) was treated as the dependent variable and regressed on total employment in 1968 as a percentage of the 1959 employment, to yield a value of $r^2$ of only $0.003$ (F $= 0.167$). This result is not acceptable at any reasonable level of significance.

Although overall there is no relationship between change in total employment and change in the Tress scores, the picture is somewhat different when the sub-regions are divided into those with above-average and below-average growth:

sub-regions with above-average growth
$$Y = 517.987 - 3.589X \quad r^2 = 0.045 \quad F = 0.013$$
sub-regions with below-average growth (or decline)
$$Y = 1,274.877 - 11.976X \quad r^2 = 0.123 \quad F = 4.208$$

where Y is the change in Tress score and X the 1968 employment as a percentage of 1959.

The former relationship is not significant even at the 95 per cent level, whereas the latter is just acceptable at that level. In both cases, the signifiance level is much lower than when the Wilcoxon $Z$ scores were used. The second of the above equations indicates that the lower the growth rate, or greater the proportionate decline in employment, the larger is the change in Tress score between 1959 and 1968. Given that the 1968 value has been subtracted from that for 1959, this implies diversification of the employment structure. This finding is at variance with the proposition that a larger total workforce is associated with a diversified structure of industries. On the other hand, to the extent that areas of low growth or even decline have benefited from the government's regional policies, this finding is consistent with the evidence adduced in Chapter 1 and accords with the results based on the Wilcoxon $Z$ statistic. Nevertheless, the strength of the association is so low that perhaps no importance should be attached to it.

The next step was to consider more directly the question of government assistance to the sub-regions, to see whether further evidence could be adduced to test the ideas discussed in Chapter 1. Though data are available at the standard region level relating to industrial development certificates, showing the number of certificates, floor space provided and employment generated, and though data are similarly available for the value of grants and allowances, no such information has been compiled for the sub-regions. There is therefore only one way in which it is possible to make a direct assessment of the extent to which a sub-region has been aided by government policies. The geographical areas eligible for aid have varied over time but the basic unit for purposes of defining Development Districts, Development Areas, etc., has always been the Employment Exchange area. Furthermore, the sub-regions are essentially amalgamations of Exchange areas. Consequently, if it is known how long each Exchange area has been eligible for assistance and the employed population thereof is also known, it is possible to derive an 'index of assistance' that shows what proportion of the employed population has benefited and for how long.

In operational terms, the index was compiled as follows. The former Board of Trade (now Department of the Environment) compiled full details of which areas have been eligible for assistance since 1945. From these records, the period 23 July 1958 to end July 1968 was selected as most nearly matching the period for which we have employment data, given the constraints of legislative changes: the DTAC areas, forerunners of the Development Districts introduced in 1960, came into being on 23 July 1958. For each exchange area, it is possible, to the nearest whole month, to obtain the number of months for which it was designated for aid, out of the maximum possible of 120. Given also the total employment for the quarter ending June 1959 and June 1968, a mean employment figure can readily be obtained for each Exchange area. If months eligible for assistance is multiplied by mean employment, an employment-weighted measure of the time for which a sub-region has been aided can readily be compiled. Expressed as a proportion of the maximum possible assistance, the index will range from 0·0 for no aid to 100·0 for continuous help for the whole sub-region.

An assistance index compiled in this way clearly has serious limitations, of which two may be noted. The nature and value of regional aid has varied over time. Furthermore, at any one time there is considerable spatial variation in the worth of the benefits obtained. Thus, it is clearly somewhat dubious to assume that one month of eligibility has the same significance irrespective of time and place. The index also has other obvious deficiencies that need not be rehearsed here.

In practice, a simple linear regression between the change in the Tress score (152 MLH) and the assistance index proved to be not significant. Re-running the regression but for manufacturing industries only and with the incorporation of a second variable, the sub-regional Tress score for 1959, did however yield a significant relationship at the 99 per cent level:

$$Y = -2,057 - 0·494X_1 + 0·158 X_2 \quad R^2 = 0·166 \quad F = 11·542$$

where Y is the difference in Tress scores (1959 minus 1968), $X_1$ is the assistance index and $X_2$ is the 1959 Tress score.

The interpretation of this relationship is as follows. A positive value of Y indicates an increased diversification of employment. Thus, the more specialised an area in 1959, the greater its diversification, and vice versa, whereas perversely the effect of a large assistance index is apparently to increase the level of specialisation. While the former relationship is expected, the latter is in complete opposition both to *a priori* expectation and the evidence already cited in Chapter 1.

Given the clear deficiencies of the assistance index and its poor *de facto* performance, we looked for other variables that might be regarded as a surrogate for government assistance. The only variable for which data are in fact available is the floor area of industrial buildings. There are various sources of these statistics. The Ministry of Housing and Local Government (1969) published figures for the sub-regions in England and Wales showing changes in the floor area of industrial, shopping and office activities between April 1964 and March 1967. In a subsequent publication, the Department of the Environment (1972) published similar data for the floor-space stock as of April 1967 and changes to March 1968. The major problems with these data are first the restriction of the coverage to England and Wales and second the fact that 1964 is the earliest year for which the data are available. We felt that these disadvantages outweighed the benefit to be had by using figures for net change. In consequence, we used figures for the gross area of factory floor space completed, as recorded through the machinery governing the award of industrial development certificates. These data are available for all the sub-regions in Great Britain for the period 1960 to 1968 inclusive (*Abstract of Regional Statistics*, No. 6, 1970). Over the period 1960 to 1968 inclusive, the definition of industrial building has changed and there have also been changes in the threshold area at which IDC controls operate. Nevertheless, the aggregate floor area constructed over the period is a good measure of the sub-regions' success in obtaining new manufacturing employment in the context of current economic conditions and the sum of government policies. Perhaps the main weakness is that the data refer to the gross change, and so it must be borne in mind that success in getting new floor space may be offset by losses from the existing stock. The Ministry of Housing (1969) showed that in the period 1964 to 1967, additions to industrial floor space in England and Wales amounted to 148·8 million square feet, whereas losses added up to 48·6 million square feet. Bearing this proviso in mind, it is probable that the greater the volume of gross completions the greater the likelihood that there will be a change in the industrial structure and hence of the degree of employment specialisation.

Since information on the stock of industrial buildings is available only for 1967 and not for a year near the beginning of our study period, and since also these data on stock refer to sub-regions in England and Wales only, we decided to relate gross construction over the period 1960 to 1968 to the mean employment total, obtaining this as the average of employment in 1959 and 1968. In this way, we obtained the gross construction in square feet per person employed in manufacturing as our measure of success in attracting new employment. Simple correlation of this variable and the change in Tress score for manufacturing industries between 1959 and 1968 resulted in a value for $r^2$ of 0·053. Although this is a better result than was obtained using the assistance index, it is nevertheless not acceptable even at the 95 per cent level. However, a multiple correlation yielded much more encouraging results:

$$Y = -1,965 + 0·0595\,X_1 + 0·150\,X_2 \quad R^2 = 0·320 \quad F = 28·018$$

where $Y$ is the difference in Tress score for a sub-region (manufacturing industries only; 1959 minus 1968), $X_1$ is the amount of industrial building per industrial worker, in square feet, and $X_2$ is the 1959 Tress score (manufacturing industries only). The value for $R^2$, at 0·320, is highly significant and may be accepted at the 99 per cent level. (Note that the two independent variables are not correlated, the value of r being 0·104 and $r^2$ 0·010. In other words, the amount of new industrial building per worker in manufacturing employment is in no way related to the degree of specialisation exhibited by a sub-region in 1959).

Since the amount of industrial building per employed person ranged from 3.4 square feet in zone 21 to just over 318 in zones 52 and 53, the contribution of this variable to the change in Tress score is very small. However, unlike the assistance index, the sign is positive, which is what one would expect.

Though the level of explanation achieved is not very high, it looks as though the main factor affecting diversification in the period under review has been the degree of specialisation that existed in 1959. Such a conclusion implies that throughout the economy there has been a strong tendency toward the diversification of regional and sub-regional economies that has been a good deal more powerful than factors associated with government policy. Although this may be a surprising conclusion, it is at least consistent with evidence cited in Chapter 1, of a general convergence toward the national mean. In particular, Leser found that whereas in 1939 Wales was the most specialised regional economy, by 1947 this honour had been taken by the Midlands; Wales was then a close second and the South an equally close third.

With the exception of the analyses based on the assistance index and gross change in industrial floor space, attention has been concentrated upon the whole employment spectrum of 152 industries at the MLH level. Evidence has been found that the main factor determining changes in the Tress score is the degree of specialisation in 1959. For the service sector alone, change in the Tress score is not significantly related to the level of specialisation in 1959, whereas for manufacturing industry the $r^2$ value of 0.216 is acceptable at the 99 per cent level. For all employment, the 1959 Tress score 'explains' 26.2 per cent of the change between 1959 and 1968. It is not possible to examine the primary sector separately, as the number of categories is too small. However, it is quite evident that whereas specialised industrial economies have tended to diversify, the same has not been true in the service sector. To the extent that overall diversification has been greater than within manufacturing alone, this reflects mainly the run-down of primary employment (notably coal mining) and its replacement by manufacturing and service work.

**Economic vulnerability**

The concept of diversity or otherwise of employment suffers from a number of defects, not the least being that the risks attaching to specialisation are closely related to the nature of the industries in which the area specialises. In terms of the data available to us, this problem may be visualised in the following way. Suppose that a sub-region had a highly diversified employment structure but that all the industries located therein were themselves highly localised—in the extreme case being found nowhere else. If another sub-region has a similar degree of diversity but all its industries are widely spread in the rest of the country, it is probable that the second region is substantially less at risk than the former. This notion can be made operational by computing a vulnerability index in the following manner:

$$V.1. = \frac{\sum_{i=1}^{n} q_i \cdot T_i}{n}$$

where $q_i$ is the proportion of employment in industry i and $T_i$ is the national Tress statistic for that industry. In the present case, $N = 152$. The Tress score for an industry spread over sixty-one sub-regions ranges from 3,100 to 6,100, representing respectively extreme dispersal and extreme localisation. By calculating $q_i$ as a proportion of 1.0, the vulnerability index will range from just over twenty to about forty, the larger figure representing dependence upon highly localised industries. However, this range only applies to the situation in which $N = n = 152$. For most regions, n is smaller (see Figure 3.13) and therefore the range of the index is greater. Where $n = 85$, the maximum feasible score is about 72.

Figures 3.10 and 3.11 show the geographical distribution of the vulnerability index scores and suggest that several regions approach the maximum possible score. In fact, in 1959 there were only three sub-regions in the upper quintile group for which the score exceeds sixty and of these only two are in excess of sixty-six (sub-regions fifty-two and fifty-eight, respectively central Wales and the Southern uplands of Scotland). By 1968, only the latter remained with a score in excess of sixty.

From Figures 3.10 and 3.11, it is clear that there is a large region of low vulnerability running from Merseyside–Yorkshire to the south coast, with some islands in the north-east and Scotland and (in 1968) East Anglia. Perhaps the most interesting feature, however, is the pattern of change revealed in Figure 3.12. By subtracting the 1968 index from 1959, a positive value indicates an improved situation of lower vulnerability. Virtually the whole of England along the Merseyside–London axis and including the south coast has experienced either little change or a worsened position. Much of Scotland has also suffered a worsening of the position. By contrast, most of eastern England, Wales and the depressed areas of the south-west peninsula have seen a marked reduction in their vulnerability.

Crude though the index may be, it is clear that again there is manifest not only a reduction in vulnerability but a narrowing in the sub-regional differences; the coefficient of variation has declined from 19 per cent to 14 per cent.

An alternative method for examining the same problem was tried and yielded very similar results. This method can be described as an occurrence index. Imagine a matrix $61 \times 152$, representing the industry classes (columns) in the sixty-one sub-regions (rows), comprising binary data of 1 and 0. The figure 1 means that an industry is represented by at least one employee; zero shows the entire absence of the industry in the sub-region. Thus, the row totals show the number of industries occurring in sub-regions and column totals the number of sub-regions in which an industry is located. Working along the rows, multiply each entry by the

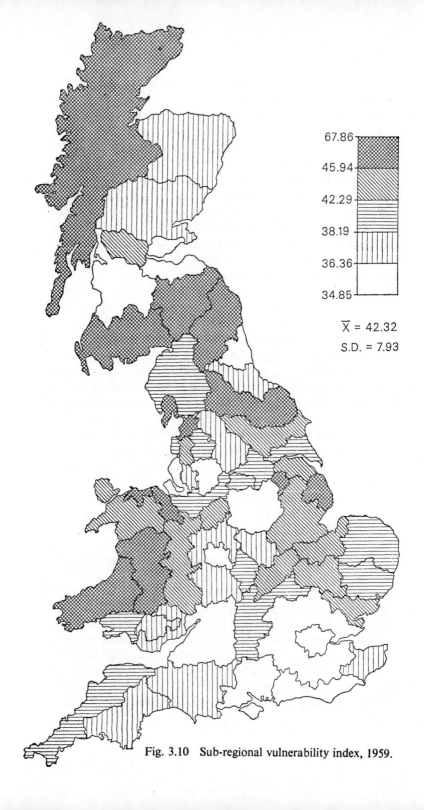

67.86
45.94
42.29
38.19
36.36
34.85

$\overline{X} = 42.32$
S.D. = 7.93

Fig. 3.10   Sub-regional vulnerability index, 1959.

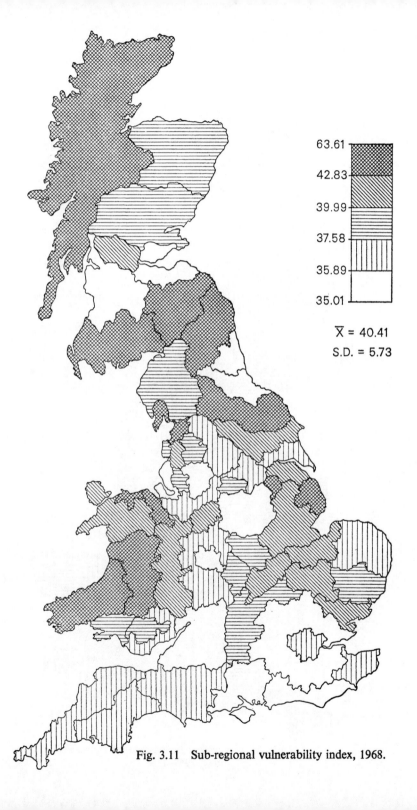

63.61
42.83
39.99
37.58
35.89
35.01

$\overline{X}$ = 40.41
S.D. = 5.73

Fig. 3.11   Sub-regional vulnerability index, 1968.

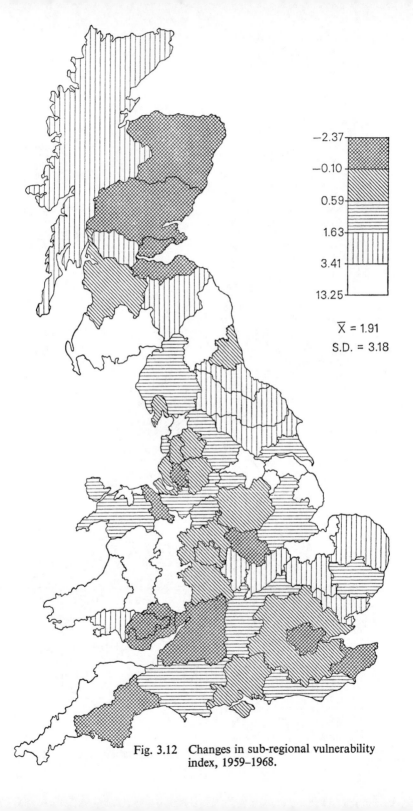

Fig. 3.12  Changes in sub-regional vulnerability index, 1959–1968.

relevant column total, sum the products and divide by the row total. The index number so obtained for each sub-region shows the mean number of times the industries occurring in the sub-region occur throughout the nation.

As the results obtained from the occurrence index are very similar to those shown by the vulnerability index, there is no need to reproduce the findings here. The important conclusion to note, however, is that the evidence for the convergence of sub-regional structures toward the national mean is robust and not unduly sensitive to the statistical technique employed.

This conclusion is yet further reinforced by simple correlation of the percentage distribution of employment among the 152 MLH industry classes in each sub-region with the national distribution. In 1959, the mean correlation coefficient (r) was 0·533 whereas by 1968 the average had risen to 0·639. This indicates clearly that the employment structures of the sub-regions are increasingly similar to the national pattern. As the standard deviations were respectively 0·274 and 0·286, the coefficient of variation has declined from 51 to 45 per cent. Thus, it is abundantly clear that there has been a general convergence of sub-regional employment structures toward the national mean.

There is one final aspect of the occurrence/non-occurrence of industries that deserves notice. We would expect sub-regions with a small total labour force to have fewer industries represented than in a sub-region of larger size. This expectation is amply confirmed by Figure 3.13. Up to about 400,000 workers, there is a linear relation between the number of industries present and the logarithm of employment. All regions in excess of this figure have an almost complete spectrum of MLH industries and there is a sharp break in the linear relationship at this level of employment. This finding should be compared with the previous conclusion that above about 1·0 million employees there is very little gain in diversification as revealed by the Tress statistic. These two findings are of course compatible but do add to our understanding of the relationship between employment total and the level of diversification. In the range below 400,000 workers, an increase in diversification associated with a larger workforce arises from two factors, an increase in the number of industries represented and greater equality of employment totals among those industries which are present. Between 0·4 and 1·0 million workers, diversification

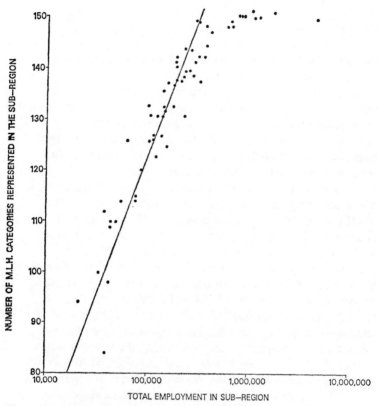

Fig. 3.13 Relationship between number of Minimum List industries and the total employment in sub-regions.

arises solely from the second cause, since all employment categories are present.

## Comparison of MLH and SIC classifications

Throughout the study so far, we have used the most highly disaggregated industrial classification available to us, namely the 152 Minimum List industries. In other studies, and especially most of those cited in Chapter 1, employment structure has been analysed in terms of the twenty-four SIC orders, of which the 152 MLH industries are sub-divisions. It is therefore of some interest to enquire whether the level of industrial disaggregation does in fact influence the results obtained.

70

To answer this question, the simplest technique is to calculate for each sub-region the Tress score using both the 24- and 152-industry classifications and to correlate the two sets so obtained. The relationship is a linear and positive one in both 1959 and 1968, but the level of correlation is really quite low: $r^2$ of 0·606 in 1959 and 0·573 in 1968. No formal test of significance is warranted, given that the sets of Tress scores are not independent of each other. But it is striking that such a large proportion of the variation in one variable is not 'explained' by the other—respectively 39 per cent and 43 per cent. This indicates very clearly that the level of industrial disaggregation does make a manifest difference to the results obtained. Since the MLH industries are more nearly homogeneous than are the SIC orders, it has seemed preferable to base our analysis on the former set, despite the greater labour involved. But the second and perhaps more interesting point to note is that over time the results from the use of SIC and MLH industries are becoming *less* similar—the value of $r^2$ has declined. If this trend should continue, it will clearly have very important consequences for regional analysis, as it implies that with the passage of time aggregation to twenty-four industries involves an increasing loss of information.

**Table 3.1** Comparison of results for sub-regional specialisation in south-east England.

| Sub-region (Project Code No.) | Coefficient of specialisation 24 SIC 1966* | Tress scores 1968 | |
|---|---|---|---|
| | | 152 MLH | 24 SIC |
| 21 | 15 | 13,190 | 1,880 |
| 22 | 17 | 13,025 | 1,836 |
| 23 | 16 | 13,507 | 1,873 |
| 24 | 18 | 13,434 | 1,910 |
| 25 | 23 | 13,694 | 1,985 |
| 26 | 14 | 13,404 | 1,897 |

* South East Economic Planning Council, 1970, p.71.

It is worth turning for a moment to the study published in 1970 by the South East Economic Planning Council. They used SIC Orders for sub-regions, albeit for the year 1966, and it should be possible to compare our results with theirs. Unfortunately, the sub-regions are not identical and though they used twenty areas it is possible to make a direct comparison with only six of the areas we have used: one reason is that our sub-region number 22 is equivalent to their Outer Metropolitan zone which they sub-divided into six areas. For what the evidence is worth, it will be seen from Table 3.1 that the ranking of the six sub-regions by the co-efficient of specialisation and by the Tress statistic, whether using twenty-four or 152 industries, does not tally very well.

### Conclusion

From the preceding discussion a number of main conclusions can be drawn. First, the Wilcoxon test does not reveal many of the sub-regions as having a change in industrial structure large enough to be regarded as significant. In the context of the present study, therefore, the two-stage mode of analysis originally envisaged proved not to be feasible and reliance has been placed mainly on the Tress statistic. Perhaps the chief reason for the rather disappointing results from the use of the Wilcoxon test lies in the relatively short time-period covered by our study.

The evidence points conclusively to the fact that in the period 1959 to 1968 there was a convergence of sub-regional employment structures toward the national mean. This is manifest in a variety of ways. Correlation of the percentage distribution of employment in the sub-regions with the national employment pattern (p.69) shows a higher mean correlation and lower coefficient of variation in the later than in the earlier year. Though the mean Tress score has hardly changed, the coefficient of variation has dropped dramatically (p.47), though note that diversification has been a feature of manufacturing industry, in contrast to the service sector, where greater areal specialisation has been characteristic (p.51). Our attempts to account for the spatial patterns of change have met with only limited success. In particular, we have found scant evidence to support the proposition made in Chapter 1 that the sub-regions in Development Areas and other assisted areas could be expected to show a disproportionate degree of diversification.

This result may be due to the crudeness of the measures we possess for identifying the amount of government aid received in the sub-regions. However, it seems more plausible to suggest that nationwide there have been strong forces at work leading to convergence in the level of employment specialisation and that government intervention has had relatively little impact. Of the independent variables available to us, the one which appears to have been the most important, albeit its explanatory power is low, is the Tress score in 1959. The regressions reported on pp.61–63 show that the higher the Tress score in 1959 (the greater the degree of specialisation) the more diversification took place. On the basis of this conclusion, we are entitled to say of government policy for diversification of the depressed areas that at least it has been working with, not against, the general run of events.

A subsidiary conclusion of some general importance for the analysis of economic development is the low and deteriorating relationship between results obtained when the 152 MLH and the twenty-four SIC industry classes are used as the basis for study. The fundamental problem here is that there are no obvious criteria by which to decide that one level of aggregation is superior to another in a given context. Perhaps the remedy for this is to perform a sensitivity analysis, whereby the robustness or otherwise of conclusions is tested by examining the effect of using various levels of aggregation.

Finally, changes in the degree of sub-regional specialisation imply shifts in the location of industries. Some industries have received more government aid than others, some have grown and some have declined. Is there any pattern that can be detected in the changing localisation of industries which will deepen our understanding of the spatial changes that have been discussed in this chapter? It is to this question that we turn in Chapter 4.

# Chapter 4  The Changing Distribution of Industries

From the evidence discussed in the previous chapter, it is abundantly clear that there has been a general tendency for the employment structures of the sub-regions to converge towards the national pattern, with a general but slight tendency to overall diversification. This behaviour of the sub-regional economies may arise from the tendency of individual industries to become more dispersed, or may be manifest despite increased localisation of industries (see Table 1.5 and accompanying text). In this chapter, we examine the behaviour of the individual industries and the general conclusion that clearly emerges is that industries have tended to become more widely distributed among the sixty-one economic planning sub-regions, over the period 1959 to 1968.

## The pattern of localisation in 1968

Table 4.1 lists the 152 MLH industries according to their Tress scores for 1968 and displays a very considerable range in the degree of localisation; the maximum and minimum scores being respectively 5,991 for the manufacture of fur and 4,584 for agriculture and horticulture. (The theoretical range is from 3,100 to 6,100.) Inspection of this table reveals that in general the manufacturing industries are at the top (localised) and services at the bottom (dispersed), a fact that is strikingly revealed in Table 4.2. Of the thirty-seven service employments, twenty-five are in the two bottom quintiles, whereas manufacturing industries almost monopolise the top quintile group.

Given the considerable variation in the degree of localisation of industries and the contrast between the manufacturing and service sectors, it is clearly important to establish whether there are any factors that can be associated with the observed Tress scores. Table 4.1 includes information on two variables that may be presumed to have a bearing on industrial localisation, namely total employment and change in employment. As initial hypotheses, it may be supposed that the larger an industry is the more likely it is to be widely dispersed. Similarly, given government control over

**Table 4.1** 1968 Tress scores for Minimum List Industries, ranked from high to low scores.

| Project Code No. | MLH Industry | | Tress score | Total employment 000, 1968 | 1968 employment as % of 1959 |
|---|---|---|---|---|---|
| 84 | 433 | Fur | 5,991 | 7·8 | 87·6 |
| 63 | 392 | Cutlery | 5,984 | 13·1 | 129·0 |
| 57 | 382 | Motor cycle, three-wheel vehicle, etc. manufacture | 5,965 | 22·8 | 62·3 |
| 72 | 414 | Woollen and worsted | 5,948 | 153·6 | 77·9 |
| 125 | 706 | Air transport | 5,918 | 62·9 | 172·1 |
| 74 | 416 | Rope, twine and net | 5,905 | 9·3 | 69·9 |
| 67 | 396 | Jewellery, plate and refining precious metals | 5,901 | 25·3 | 88·5 |
| 73 | 415 | Jute | 5,876 | 15·6 | 88·8 |
| 47 | 352 | Watches and clocks | 5,866 | 13·9 | 93·7 |
| 77 | 419 | Carpets | 5,859 | 42·0 | 126·4 |
| 76 | 418 | Lace | 5,851 | 8·0 | 88·2 |
| 22 | 262 | Mineral oil refining | 5,843 | 32·1 | 78·6 |
| 94 | 462 | Pottery | 5,842 | 58·7 | 87·1 |
| 64 | 393 | Bolts, nuts, screws, rivets, etc. | 5,838 | 45·6 | 111·6 |
| 62 | 391 | Tools and implements | 5,837 | 22·1 | 97·2 |
| 70 | 412 | Spinning and doubling of fibres | 5,831 | 84·4 | 62·1 |
| 39 | 335 | Textile machinery and accessories | 5,818 | 45·8 | 95·0 |
| 31 | 312 | Steel tubes | 5,801 | 52·9 | 102·6 |
| 90 | 446 | Hats, caps and millinery | 5,792 | 9·8 | 62·5 |
| 87 | 443 | Women's and girls' tailored outerwear | 5,792 | 61·4 | 92·4 |
| 75 | 417 | Hosiery and other knitted goods | 5,788 | 126·9 | 109·8 |
| 20 | 240 | Tobacco | 5,787 | 39·1 | 96·6 |
| 110 | 492 | Linoleum, leather cloth, etc. | 5,785 | 13·4 | 72·8 |
| 61 | 389 | Perambulators, hand trucks, etc. | 5,784 | 5·4 | 71·4 |
| 49 | 362 | Insulated wires and cables | 5,775 | 55·1 | 91·6 |
| 13 | 216 | Sugar | 5,772 | 15·1 | 81·6 |
| 85 | 441 | Weatherproof outerwear | 5,770 | 26·1 | 88·9 |
| 23 | 263 | Lubricating oils and greases | 5,751 | 8·3 | 90·7 |
| 55 | 370/2 | Marine engineering | 5,748 | 38·4 | 50·8 |
| 59 | 384 | Locomotives and railway track equipment | 5,744 | 27·9 | 38·9 |
| 80 | 423 | Textile finishing | 5,744 | 63·4 | 77·2 |
| 27 | 275 | Vegetable and animal oils, fats, etc. | 5,725 | 34·7 | 87·2 |
| 50 | 363 | Telegraph and telephone apparatus | 5,721 | 90·4 | 158·0 |
| 137 | 475 | Religious organisations | 5,711 | 20·6 | 99·2 |
| 29 | 277 | Polishes, gelatine, adhesives, etc. | 5,710 | 13·8 | 115·0 |
| 71 | 413 | Weaving of cotton, linen, etc., fibres | 5,708 | 73·8 | 59·5 |
| 126 | 707 | Postal services and telecommunications | 5,703 | 191·9 | 116·5 |

| Project Code No. | MLH Industry | | Tress score | Total employment 000, 1968 | 1968 employment as % of 1959 |
|---|---|---|---|---|---|
| 42 | 338 | Office machinery | 5,703 | 48·7 | 91·5 |
| 113 | 495 | Miscellaneous stationers' goods | 5,702 | 12·0 | 101·2 |
| 10 | 213 | Biscuits | 5,695 | 52·3 | 92·4 |
| 21 | 261 | Coke ovens and manufactured fuel | 5,691 | 16·6 | 83·7 |
| 78 | 421 | Narrow fabrics | 5,688 | 20·8 | 98·8 |
| 95 | 463 | Glass | 5,687 | 80·8 | 105·8 |
| 112 | 494 | Toys, games and sports equipment | 5,687 | 39·2 | 135·8 |
| 3 | 003 | Fishing | 5,681 | 20·9 | 79·2 |
| 45 | 324/49 | Ordnance, small arms and other mechanical engineering n.e.s. | 5,669 | 508·3 | 233·2 |
| 46 | 351 | Scientific, surgical and photographic instruments, etc. | 5,664 | 132·2 | 115·6 |
| 123 | 704 | Sea transport | 5,659 | 82·3 | 66·2 |
| 124 | 705 | Port and inland water transport | 5,650 | 134·5 | 88·2 |
| 38 | 334 | Industrial engines | 5,648 | 37.6 | 105·9 |
| 7 | 109 | 'Other' mining and quarrying | 5,644 | 11·1 | 68·6 |
| 26 | 274 | Paint and printing ink | 5,637 | 43·6 | 90·9 |
| 34 | 322 | Copper, brass and other base metals | 5,634 | 84·9 | 113·3 |
| 25 | 272 | Pharmaceutical and toilet preparations | 5,633 | 79·2 | 114·8 |
| 30 | 311 | Iron and steel (general) | 5,626 | 279·2 | 100·5 |
| 68 | 399 | Metal industries n.e.s. | 5,616 | 388·5 | 116·8 |
| 106 | 483 | Manuf. of paper and board n.e.s. | 5,615 | 72·0 | 113·9 |
| 83 | 432 | Leather goods | 5,602 | 23·1 | 99·8 |
| 4 | 101 | Coal mining | 5,600 | 443·1 | 57·6 |
| 81 | 429 | 'Other' textile industries | 5,593 | 25·6 | 96·7 |
| 54 | 370/1 | Shipbuilding and ship-repairing | 5,591 | 154·0 | 76·1 |
| 33 | 321 | Light metals | 5,583 | 58·6 | 102·9 |
| 138 | 879 | 'Other' professional and scientific services | 5,581 | 188·4 | 145·6 |
| 101 | 474 | Shop and office fitting | 5,571 | 38·8 | 158·9 |
| 69 | 411 | Production of man-made fibres | 5,570 | 42·7 | 110·5 |
| 149 | 899 | 'Other' services | 5,560 | 456·7 | 175·1 |
| 37 | 333 | Engineers' small tools and gauges | 5,550 | 70·6 | 158·9 |
| 60 | 385 | Railway carriages and wagons and trams | 5,548 | 31·7 | 40·5 |
| 66 | 395 | Cans and metal boxes | 5,545 | 33·9 | 100·4 |
| 86 | 442 | Men's and boys' tailored outerwear | 5,544 | 109·4 | 86·4 |
| 53 | 369 | 'Other' electrical goods | 5,543 | 151·3 | 117·0 |
| 92 | 450 | Footwear | 5,541 | 96·2 | 84·7 |
| 132 | 860 | Insurance, banking and finance | 5,531 | 648·5 | 125·1 |
| 139 | 881 | Cinemas, theatres, radio, etc. | 5,523 | 124·4 | 87·8 |
| 127 | 709 | Misc. transport services and storage | 5,522 | 81·7 | 127·1 |
| 96 | 464 | Cement | 5,521 | 17·3 | 108·8 |
| 58 | 383 | Aircraft manuf. and repairing | 5,519 | 242·1 | 87·2 |

| Project Code No. | MLH Industry | | Tress score | Total employment 000, 1968 | 1968 employment as % of 1959 |
|---|---|---|---|---|---|
| 51 | 364 | Radio and other electronic apparatus | 5,515 | 336·0 | 157·5 |
| 107 | 486 | Printing, publishing of newspapers, etc. | 5,513 | 141·9 | 112·7 |
| 89 | 445 | Dresses, lingerie, infants' wear, etc. | 5,508 | 110·9 | 100·7 |
| 111 | 493 | Brushes and brooms | 5,503 | 12·2 | 76·7 |
| 65 | 394 | Wire and wire manufactures | 5,501 | 42·3 | 100·6 |
| 150 | 901 | National government service | 5,492 | 319·8 | 106·7 |
| 104 | 481 | Paper and board | 5,485 | 92·7 | 100·7 |
| 128 | 810 | Wholesale distribution | 5,472 | 484·9 | 99·1 |
| 79 | 422 | Made-up textiles | 5,466 | 29·8 | 95·5 |
| 36 | 332 | Metal-working machine tools | 5,465 | 97·1 | 112·4 |
| 115 | 499 | Miscellaneous manufacturing industries | 5,463 | 40·9 | 100·2 |
| 14 | 217 | Cocoa, chocolate and sugar confectionery | 5,457 | 87·3 | 88·2 |
| 56 | 381 | Motor vehicle manufacturing | 5,448 | 476·2 | 124·1 |
| 41 | 337 | Mechanical handling equipment | 5,436 | 59·0 | 120·9 |
| 147 | 889 | Hairdressing and manicure | 5,434 | 98·5 | 130·0 |
| 91 | 449 | Dress industries n.e.s. | 5,431 | 37·2 | 93·3 |
| 109 | 491 | Rubber | 5,425 | 127·3 | 107·3 |
| 100 | 473 | Bedding, etc. | 5,421 | 19·4 | 96·7 |
| 88 | 444 | Overalls and men's shirts, underwear, etc. | 5,420 | 40·2 | 82·4 |
| 142 | 884 | Catering, hotels, etc. | 5,416 | 580·0 | 102·6 |
| 108 | 489 | 'Other' printing, publishing, etc. | 5,410 | 262·5 | 114·6 |
| 52 | 365 | Domestic electrical appliances | 5,406 | 59·1 | 102·3 |
| 40 | 336 | Contractors' plant and quarrying machinery | 5,398 | 40·1 | 160·1 |
| 114 | 496 | Plastics moulding and fabricating | 5,388 | 104·7 | 191·8 |
| 152 | — | Ex-service personnel | 5,387 | 1·9 | 32·7 |
| 151 | 906 | Local government service | 5,386 | 843·9 | 114·6 |
| 117 | 601 | Gas | 5,380 | 126·6 | 95·6 |
| 145 | 887 | Motor repairers, distributors, etc. | 5,379 | 419·2 | 125·2 |
| 28 | 276 | Synthetic resins and plastics materials | 5,365 | 39·7 | 174·1 |
| 48 | 361 | Electrical machinery | 5,364 | 210·6 | 101·2 |
| 146 | 888 | Repair of boots and shoes | 5,358 | 9·3 | 51·1 |
| 44 | 341 | Industrial plant and steelwork | 5,350 | 182·4 | 123·5 |
| 82 | 431 | Leather and fellmongery | 5,331 | 25·4 | 80·1 |
| 32 | 313 | Iron castings, etc. | 5,331 | 111·0 | 91·4 |
| 103 | 479 | Miscellaneous wood and cork manufacturing | 5,320 | 21·3 | 103·5 |
| 19 | 239 | 'Other' drink industries | 5,312 | 67·3 | 110·9 |
| 99 | 472 | Furniture and upholstery | 5,307 | 101·4 | 98·1 |
| 105 | 482 | Cardboard boxes, cartons, etc. | 5,304 | 63·1 | 104·9 |

| Project Code No. | MLH Industry | | Tress score | Total employment 000, 1968 | 1968 employment as % of 1959 |
|---|---|---|---|---|---|
| 131 | 832 | Dealing in 'other' industrial materials and machinery | 5,300 | 129·7 | 111·1 |
| 135 | 873 | Legal services | 5,291 | 108·8 | 131·3 |
| 16 | 219 | Animal and poultry foods | 5,278 | 25·6 | 128·8 |
| 12 | 215 | Milk products | 5,274 | 35·6 | 90·6 |
| 130 | 831 | Dealings in coal, builders' materials, etc. | 5,264 | 121·3 | 77·7 |
| 102 | 475 | Wooden containers and baskets | 5,252 | 25·4 | 99·6 |
| 133 | 871 | Accountancy services | 5,249 | 91·1 | 118·1 |
| 43 | 339 | 'Other' machinery | 5,244 | 354·8 | 111·6 |
| 15 | 218 | Fruit and vegetable products | 5,242 | 71·9 | 99·9 |
| 97 | 469 | Abrasives and building materials n.e.s. | 5,236 | 128·9 | 138·5 |
| 141 | 883 | Betting | 5,229 | 56·7 | 152·8 |
| 93 | 461 | Bricks, fireclay and refractory goods | 5,218 | 66·4 | 88·3 |
| 17 | 229 | Food industries n.e.s. | 5,218 | 50·8 | 134·2 |
| 120 | 701 | Railways | 5,206 | 293·8 | 62·3 |
| 129 | 820 | Retail distribution | 5,146 | 1,827·3 | 101·2 |
| 116 | 500 | Construction | 5,130 | 1,549·4 | 111·1 |
| 18 | 231 | Brewing and malting | 5,124 | 89·1 | 93·8 |
| 11 | 214 | Bacon curing, meat and fish products | 5,116 | 88·8 | 138·2 |
| 136 | 874 | Medical and dental services | 5,109 | 958·2 | 130·9 |
| 144 | 886 | Dry cleaning, job dyeing, etc. | 5,094 | 36·3 | 84·7 |
| 35 | 331 | Agricultural machinery (except tractors) | 5,087 | 34·6 | 94·7 |
| 24 | 271/73 | Chemicals, dyes, explosives and fireworks | 5,083 | 233·4 | 95·8 |
| 118 | 602 | Electricity | 5,059 | 244·4 | 118·0 |
| 134 | 872 | Educational services | 5,057 | 1,272·6 | 150·3 |
| 6 | 103 | Chalk, clay, sand and gravel extraction | 5,052 | 24·8 | 109·8 |
| 8 | 211 | Grain milling | 5,050 | 36·8 | 90·4 |
| 121 | 702 | Road passenger transport | 5,030 | 261·8 | 95·6 |
| 9 | 212 | Bread and flour confectionery | 5,027 | 148·7 | 111·4 |
| 143 | 885 | Laundries | 5,011 | 97·4 | 75·8 |
| 140 | 882 | Sport and other recreations | 4,963 | 71·6 | 139·4 |
| 148 | 891 | Private domestic service | 4,942 | 148·8 | 50·9 |
| 5 | 102 | Stone and slate quarrying and mining | 4,898 | 21·8 | 72·3 |
| 2 | 002 | Forestry | 4,876 | 14·9 | 72·6 |
| 122 | 703 | Road haulage contracting | 4,865 | 238·6 | 130·9 |
| 119 | 603 | Water supply | 4,835 | 44·1 | 123·8 |
| 98 | 471 | Timber | 4,827 | 117·7 | 130·9 |
| 1 | 001 | Agriculture and horticulture | 4,584 | 380·4 | 69·7 |

**Table 4.2** Summary of 1968 Tress scores for Minimum List industries

| Quintile group from high score at top to low at bottom | Number of Industries | | | |
| --- | --- | --- | --- | --- |
| | Primary 001–109 | Manufacturing 211–499 | Services 500–906 | Total |
| 1st | 0 | 30 | 1 | 31 |
| 2nd | 3 | 23 | 4 | 30 |
| 3rd | 0 | 23 | 7 | 30 |
| 4th | 0 | 20 | 10 | 30 |
| 5th | 4 | 12 | 15 | 31 |
| Total | 7 | 108 | 37 | 152 |

Source: Table 4.1

industrial location, it is reasonable to expect fast growing industries to be more widely dispersed than slow growing or declining ones. In practice, it is of course more reasonable to suggest that these two factors operate simultaneously.

This hypothesis was only partially confirmed. Growth was measured by taking the 1968 employment as a percentage of the 1959 level, but proved not to be a significant factor: nevertheless, the sign of the coefficient was negative, which is at least the direction that would be expected. With growth rate eliminated as a non-significant variable, it was found that localisation is in fact related to the total employment in the industry, in the following manner:

$$Y = 5587 \cdot 90 - 0 \cdot 0004705X \quad r^2 = 0 \cdot 129 \quad F = 22 \cdot 204$$

where Y is the 1968 Tress score for an industry and X the total employment, also for 1968. This result is acceptable at the 99 per cent level of significance, but does not represent a very high level of explanation. The poor performance of the equation could be due to non-linearity in the relationship and therefore we carried out the following further analysis. The data were divided into a $2 \times 2$ contingency table, using the mean values of X and Y as the dividing lines. Regressions were then run for the four data sets but in no case was an association established that can be accepted even at the 95 per cent level. This result indicates that there is no element of non-linearity in the over-all set of observations for the 152 MLH industries, and thus shows that there is nothing to be gained from attempting to fit equations more elaborate than the one reported above.

From these analyses, therefore, we can conclude that there is a statistically significant, but slight, tendency for the larger industries to be more widely dispersed geographically than smaller ones. As for the rate of growth, this appears not to be relevant, which might imply that government policies have had no detectable impact on the over-all degree of localisation. However, it is just possible that this is because the time period of our study is too short: the sign of the coefficient was negative, as expected, and so it may be that a longer span of years would have yielded a significant relationship.

Further information relevant to patterns of localisation is contained in the 1963 census of manufacturing. In the first place, we can ascertain the number of establishments in each MLH manufacturing industry. Now there are two alternative ways in which the number of plants may be related to the geographical distribution. In the first place, a small number of plants implies that each sells at least over a regional, if not a national or international market. In this case, the plants may either be located in one area, or highly dispersed in relation to specific locational factors, such as deep water access. At the other extreme, small but numerous plants may reflect a wide dispersal in relation to markets, as with the manufacture of mineral waters, or highly specialised processing of components that requires plants to be localised near their main customers. Thus, there is no *a priori* reason to expect industries with many (few) plants to be geographically dispersed (localised). On the other hand, where transport costs are significant, we would expect plants to be widely dispersed to minimise the penalties of high transport costs on long hauls.

After a certain amount of experiment, the first of the two above propositions was confirmed: the extent of geographical localisation is not significantly related to the number of plants in the industry. On the other hand, there is some association with transport costs significant at the 99 per cent level, as shown by the following equation for the manufacturing industries:

$$Y = 5{,}924 - 17{\cdot}902\,X_1 - 2{\cdot}583\,X_2 \quad R^2 = 0{\cdot}241 \quad F = 33{\cdot}66$$

where $Y$ = the 1968 Tress score
$\quad\quad X_1$ = transport costs as a percentage of net output
$\quad\quad X_2$ = employment in 1968 as a percentage of 1959

Estimates of transport costs ($X_1$) have been taken from Edwards (1970) and are based on the 1963 census. Percentage change in employment has been calculated from the data supplied by the Department of Employment. The nature of the relationship is as we would expect. Where costs of transport are high relative to net output, the Tress score is lower, indicating wide dispersal. Similarly, dispersal is associated with positive growth in employment, whereas negative growth seems to lead to some increase in localisation. However, since less than a quarter of the variance is explained by the two independent variables, the strength of the association must not be overrated.

## The Wilcoxon test for changing localisation

The Wilcoxon test can be used to see whether there has been a statistically significant change in the distribution of each industry among the sixty-one sub-regions; the results of this test are shown in Table 4.3. For only fifteen industries has the change been significant at the 99 per cent level, though in another nineteen cases the change may be accepted at the 95 per cent level. In the other 118 cases, changes in the spatial distributions have been too small to be regarded as anything but random by this test.

Table 4.3 displays some notable features. In the first place, none of the primary industries is included among the thirty-four industries listed. The second feature is the fact that even if ex-service personnel is excluded as being a special category, the service employments are over-represented in this table. They account for one-third of the industries listed, whereas among the total of 151 industries (ex-service personnel excluded) they represent only 24 per cent of the industries. There is thus some propensity for the service industries to change spatial distributions more readily than manufacturing industries.

The third feature of Table 4.3 is the fact that though some quite small industries are included, many may be regarded as medium-sized and several as large. Thus, significant locational changes are not confined to the industries employing small numbers. It is also noteworthy that significant change is found where growth or decline has been only moderate as well as where it has been very great. In other words, significant changes in

81

**Table 4.3**  Wilcoxon test for locational changes for Minimum List industries

| Level of significance of structural change | Project Code No. | Industry MLH Number | Name | Total employment, 000, 1968 | 1968 employment, as % of 1959 |
|---|---|---|---|---|---|
| 99% and over | 17 | 229 | Food n.e.s. | 50·8 | 134·2 |
| | 19 | 239 | 'Other' drink | 67·3 | 110·9 |
| | 22 | 262 | Oil refining | 32·1 | 78·6 |
| | 31 | 312 | Steel tubes | 52·9 | 102·6 |
| | 37 | 333 | Small tools and gauges | 70·6 | 158·9 |
| | 38 | 334 | Industrial engines | 37·6 | 105·9 |
| | 43 | 339 | 'Other' machinery | 354·8 | 111·6 |
| | 45 | 342/49 | Arms, and engineering n.e.s. | 508·3 | 232·2 |
| | 48 | 361 | Electrical machinery | 210·6 | 101·2 |
| | 50 | 363 | Telegraph and telephone apparatus | 90·4 | 158·0 |
| | 68 | 399 | Metal industries n.e.s. | 388·5 | 116·8 |
| | 137 | 875 | Religious organisations | 20·6 | 99·2 |
| | 142 | 884 | Catering, hotels, etc. | 580·0 | 102·6 |
| | 146 | 888 | Repair of boots and shoes | 9·3 | 51·1 |
| | 152 | – | Ex-service personnel | 1·9 | 32·7 |

| | | | | |
|---|---|---|---|---|
| 20 | 240 | Tobacco | 39·1 | 96·6 |
| 23 | 263 | Lubricating oils and greases | 8·3 | 90·7 |
| 42 | 338 | Office machinery | 48·7 | 91·5 |
| 49 | 362 | Insulated wires and cables | 55·1 | 91·6 |
| 52 | 365 | Domestic electric appliances | 59·1 | 102·3 |
| 53 | 369 | 'Other' electrical goods | 151·3 | 117·0 |
| 64 | 393 | Bolts, nuts, screws, etc | 45·6 | 111·6 |
| 70 | 412 | Spinning and doubling of fibres | 84·4 | 62·1 |
| 72 | 414 | Woollen and worsted | 153·6 | 77·9 |
| 101 | 474 | Shop and office fitting | 38·8 | 158·9 |
| 114 | 496 | Plastics moulding and fabricating | 104·7 | 191·8 |
| 117 | 601 | Gas | 126·6 | 95·6 |
| 130 | 831 | Dealing in coal, materials, etc. | 121·3 | 77·7 |
| 135 | 873 | Legal services | 108·8 | 131·3 |
| 143 | 885 | Laundries | 97·4 | 75·8 |
| 145 | 887 | Motor repair, garages, etc. | 419·2 | 125·2 |
| 147 | 889 | Hairdressing and manicure | 98·5 | 130·0 |
| 148 | 891 | Private domestic service | 148·8 | 50·9 |
| 151 | 906 | Local government service | 843·9 | 114·6 |

distribution occur in situations of rapid decline in employment, rapid growth and also where the growth in some sub-regions is roughly offset by decline elsewhere.

Perhaps the most notable feature of Table 4.3, however, is the absence of one or two industries that it is generally thought have been greatly affected by government regional policy. The manufacture of vehicles is the outstanding case, with the large-scale development of plants both in Merseyside and Scotland from the early 1960s, at considerable public expense. This point is strikingly made by comparison of Table 4.3 with Table 1.2. The latter shows, for the SIC Orders, the proportion of employment in individual industries that was accounted for by plants mobile in the period 1945–65. This proportion exceeded 10 per cent in five of the Orders and it would be reasonable to expect that the MLH industries which comprise these Orders would figure prominently in Table 4.3. Only for Order VI (Engineering and electrical goods) is this expectation borne out; ten of the twenty-two manufacturing industries in Table 4.3 are in this Order. On the other hand, Orders VIII (Vehicles) and XII (Clothing and footwear) are not represented in Table 4.3. Thus, most especially in the case of vehicles but also of other industries, a high level of plant mobility does not seem to be associated with increased geographical dispersal of employment. Whatever else may have been achieved, it would appear that there has not been a net dispersal of the manufacture of vehicles, for example, however significant the new plants may be within their respective local economies.

Setting aside the question whether the Wilcoxon results are statistically significant, it is again useful to treat the $Z$ scores as the dependent variable. Dividing the industries into those which declined or grew less than average and those which expanded above average, an entirely non-significant relationship between the $Z$ score and rate of decline is manifest. However, for the growing industries, there is a positive relationship yielding an $r^2$ of 0·124 ($F = 10·987$), which is acceptable at the 99 per cent level. This suggests a tendency for rapidly growing industries to be changing their pattern of location more than slower growing ones, though the tendency is clearly not very marked. Interestingly enough, this conclusion is the reverse of that obtained in examining the $Z$ scores for the sub-regions (p.44); there is no clear reason why this difference should be manifest.

As in Chapter 3, the results of the Wilcoxon test are not very helpful and therefore it is useful to turn to the Tress statistic to probe matters further.

### The changing localisation of industry

Table 4.4. shows the change in Tress scores for the 152 MLH industries, with the industries ranked from the highest positive value downwards. As the 1968 score has been subtracted from the 1959 one, a positive value indicates an increase in diversification, whereas a negative change shows that greater localisation has occurred. We would expect the industries listed in Table 4.3 to appear at the top and the bottom of Table 4.4, i.e. that where the Wilcoxon test shows a significant change in structure a large positive or negative change in the Tress score would have occurred. This expectation is only partially borne out in practice, thus confirming what was shown in Chapter 3, namely that the correlation between change measured by Wilcoxon $Z$ statistic and by the Tress score is not especially high.

A noteworthy point shown by Table 4.4 is that the change in Tress score (1959 minus 1968) was positive for 100 industries and negative in fifty-one cases; for one industry, the change was zero when results are rounded to the nearest whole number. This indicates clearly that the preponderant change has been toward greater geographical dispersion. The unweighted mean score was 5,523 in 1959 and 5,485 in 1968; in the notation we have used, this is a positive shift of thirty-eight in the Tress score. Thus, over-all there has been a slight tendency for industries to become less localised.

Equally striking is the distribution of the three broad classes of employment that may be labelled 'primary', 'manufacturing' and 'service'. In general, the primary industries of agriculture, forestry, fishing, mining and quarrying appear in the lower half of Table 4.4, as is clearly shown in Table 4.5, and are thus generally characterised by increasing localisation. The same phenomenon is evident for the service industries, with twenty-four of the thirty-seven occurring in the two lower quintiles (Tables 4.4 and 4.5). On the other hand, the manufacturing sector is composed of industries which in general are becoming geographically more dispersed. Thus, if the mean change in Tress score and standard

**Table 4.4** Changes in Tress scores for Minimum List industries, ranked from high positive to high negative change (1959 minus 1968).

| Project Code No. | Industry MLH No. | | Change in Tress score | Total employment '000, 1959 | 1968 employment as % of 1959 | 1959 Tress score |
|---|---|---|---|---|---|---|
| 141 | 883 | Betting | +368 | 37·1 | 152·8 | 5,597 |
| 152 | – | Ex-service personnel | +359 | 5·8 | 32·7 | 5,746 |
| 17 | 229 | Food industries n.e.s. | +346 | 37·9 | 134·2 | 5,563 |
| 114 | 496 | Plastics moulding and fabricating | +271 | 54·6 | 191·8 | 5,659 |
| 40 | 336 | Contractors' plant and quarrying machinery | +256 | 25·1 | 160·1 | 5,654 |
| 28 | 276 | Synthetic resins and plastics materials | +241 | 22·8 | 174·1 | 5,606 |
| 96 | 464 | Cement | +210 | 15·9 | 108·8 | 5,730 |
| 50 | 363 | Telegraph and telephone apparatus | +207 | 57·2 | 158·0 | 5,928 |
| 101 | 474 | Shop and office fitting | +191 | 24·4 | 158·9 | 5,762 |
| 98 | 471 | Timber | +185 | 89·9 | 130·9 | 5,012 |
| 115 | 499 | Miscellaneous manuf. industries | +179 | 40·9 | 100·2 | 5,642 |
| 105 | 482 | Cardboard, boxes, cartons, etc. | +175 | 60·1 | 104·9 | 5,479 |
| 99 | 472 | Furniture and upholstery | +169 | 103·4 | 98·1 | 5,476 |
| 37 | 333 | Engineers' small tools and gauges | +165 | 44·4 | 158·9 | 5,715 |
| 48 | 361 | Electrical machinery | +165 | 208·2 | 101·2 | 5,528 |
| 119 | 603 | Water supply | +161 | 35·6 | 123·8 | 4,995 |

| | | | | | | |
|---|---|---|---|---|---|---|
| 16 | 219 | Animal and poultry foods | +159 | 19·9 | 128·8 | 5,438 |
| 102 | 475 | Wooden containers and baskets | +158 | 25·5 | 99·6 | 5,410 |
| 52 | 365 | Domestic electric appliances | +151 | 57·7 | 102·3 | 5,558 |
| 90 | 446 | Hats, caps and millinery | +151 | 15·7 | 62·5 | 5,943 |
| 44 | 341 | Industrial plant and steelwork | +151 | 147·6 | 123·5 | 5,500 |
| 56 | 381 | Motor vehicle manufacturing | +144 | 383·9 | 124·1 | 5,592 |
| 51 | 364 | Radio and other electronic apparatus | +141 | 213·3 | 157·5 | 5,656 |
| 73 | 415 | Jute | +140 | 17·6 | 88·8 | 6,016 |
| 43 | 339 | 'Other' machinery | +139 | 317·9 | 111·6 | 5,383 |
| 113 | 495 | Miscellaneous stationers' goods | +132 | 11·9 | 101·2 | 5,835 |
| 92 | 450 | Footwear | +128 | 113·6 | 84·7 | 5,669 |
| 106 | 483 | Manufacture of paper and board n.e.s. | +128 | 63·2 | 113·9 | 5,743 |
| 144 | 886 | Dry cleaning, job dyeing, etc. | +123 | 42·9 | 84·7 | 5,217 |
| 24 | 271 and 273 | Chemicals, dyes, explosives and fireworks | +122 | 243·5 | 95·8 | 5,205 |
| 42 | 338 | Office machinery | +121 | 53·2 | 91·5 | 5,824 |
| 53 | 369 | 'Other' electrical goods | +119 | 129·3 | 117·0 | 5,662 |
| 83 | 432 | Leather goods | +119 | 23·2 | 99·8 | 5,721 |
| 85 | 441 | Weatherproof outerwear | +113 | 29·4 | 88·9 | 5,883 |
| 100 | 473 | Bedding, etc. | +111 | 20·1 | 96·7 | 5,533 |
| 76 | 418 | Lace | +111 | 9·1 | 88·2 | 5,962 |
| 46 | 352 | Watches and clocks | +109 | 114·4 | 115·6 | 5,773 |
| 122 | 703 | Road haulage contracting | +105 | 182·4 | 130·9 | 4,970 |
| 94 | 462 | Pottery | +104 | 67·4 | 87·1 | 5,955 |

| Project Code No. | Industry MLH No. | | Change in Tress score | Total employment '000, 1959 | 1968 employment as % of 1959 | 1959 Tress score |
|---|---|---|---|---|---|---|
| 95 | 463 | Glass | +101 | 76·4 | 105·8 | 5,788 |
| 71 | 413 | Weaving of cotton, linen, etc., fibres | +100 | 124·2 | 59·5 | 5,808 |
| 109 | 491 | Rubber | +100 | 118·6 | 107·3 | 5,524 |
| 81 | 429 | 'Other' textile industries | +89 | 26·4 | 96·7 | 5,682 |
| 11 | 214 | Bacon curing, meat and fish products | +89 | 64·3 | 138·2 | 5,205 |
| 41 | 337 | Mechanical handling | +87 | 48·8 | 120·9 | 5,524 |
| 88 | 444 | Overalls and men's shirts, etc. | +86 | 48·7 | 82·4 | 5,506 |
| 89 | 445 | Dresses, lingerie, infants' wear, etc. | +85 | 110·2 | 100·7 | 5,593 |
| 123 | 704 | Sea transport | +82 | 124·3 | 66·2 | 5,741 |
| 148 | 891 | Private domestic service | +80 | 292·3 | 50·9 | 5,022 |
| 77 | 419 | Carpets | +78 | 33·2 | 126·4 | 5,937 |
| 87 | 443 | Women's and girls' tailored outerwear | +77 | 66·4 | 92·4 | 5,869 |
| 23 | 263 | Lubricating oils and greases | +76 | 9·2 | 90·7 | 5,827 |
| 70 | 412 | Spinning and doubling of fibres | +74 | 136·0 | 62·1 | 5,905 |
| 79 | 422 | Made-up textiles | +72 | 31·2 | 95·5 | 5,539 |
| 66 | 395 | Cans and metal boxes | +72 | 33·8 | 100·4 | 5,628 |
| 107 | 486 | Printing and publishing of newspapers and periodicals | +70 | 125·9 | 112·7 | 5,583 |
| 22 | 262 | Mineral oil refining | +69 | 40·9 | 78·6 | 5,912 |

| | | | | | |
|---|---|---|---|---|---|
| 38 | Industrial engines | + 64 | 35·5 | 105·9 | 5,711 |
| 97 | Abrasives and building materials, etc. n.e.s. | + 63 | 93·0 | 138·5 | 5,299 |
| 36 | Metal-working machine tools | + 63 | 86·3 | 112·4 | 5,528 |
| 25 | Pharmaceutical and toilet preparations | + 63 | 69·0 | 114·8 | 5,696 |
| 69 | Production of man-made fibres | + 62 | 38·6 | 110·5 | 5,632 |
| 63 | Cutlery | + 61 | 10·1 | 129·0 | 6,046 |
| 31 | Steel tubes | + 61 | 51·6 | 102·6 | 5,862 |
| 111 | Brushes and brooms | + 61 | 15·9 | 76·7 | 5,564 |
| 58 | Aircraft manufacture and repair | + 57 | 277·7 | 87·2 | 5,576 |
| 34 | Copper, brass and other base metals | + 55 | 74·9 | 113·3 | 5,689 |
| 64 | Bolts, nuts, screws, rivets, etc. | + 50 | 40·9 | 111·6 | 5,888 |
| 112 | Toys, games and sports equipment | + 45 | 28·9 | 135·8 | 5,732 |
| 67 | Jewellery, plate and refining precious metals | + 48 | 28·6 | 88·5 | 5,949 |
| 9 | Bread and flour confectionery | + 48 | 133·4 | 111·4 | 5,074 |
| 80 | Textile finishing | + 46 | 82·1 | 77·2 | 5,790 |
| 5 | Stone and slate quarrying and mining | + 45 | 30·2 | 72·3 | 4,943 |
| 49 | Insulated wires and cables | + 42 | 60·1 | 91·6 | 5,816 |
| 20 | Tobacco | + 40 | 40·5 | 96·6 | 5,827 |
| 27 | Vegetable and animal oils, fats, soap, etc. | + 39 | 39·8 | 87·2 | 5,765 |
| 128 | Wholesale distribution | + 38 | 489·3 | 99·1 | 5,510 |
| 86 | Men's and boys' tailored outerwear | + 37 | 126·6 | 86·4 | 5,581 |
| 103 | Miscellaneous wood and cork manufacture | + 35 | 20·5 | 103·5 | 5,355 |
| 62 | Tools and implements | + 35 | 22·7 | 97·2 | 5,872 |
| 116 | Construction | + 35 | 1,394·4 | 111·1 | 5,164 |

| Project Code No. | Industry MLH No. | | Change in Tress score | Total employment '000, 1959 | 1968 employment as % of 1959 | 1959 Tress score |
|---|---|---|---|---|---|---|
| 138 | 879 | 'Other' professional services | + 34 | 129·3 | 145·6 | 5,616 |
| 65 | 394 | Wire and wire manufactures | + 31 | 42·1 | 100·6 | 5,532 |
| 12 | 215 | Milk products | + 28 | 39·3 | 90·6 | 5,301 |
| 136 | 874 | Medical and dental services | + 25 | 732·1 | 130·9 | 5,134 |
| 140 | 882 | Sport and other recreations | + 23 | 51·4 | 139·4 | 4,986 |
| 72 | 414 | Woollen and worsted | + 22 | 197·3 | 77·9 | 5,970 |
| 39 | 335 | Textile machinery and accessories | + 22 | 48·2 | 95·0 | 5,840 |
| 125 | 706 | Air transport | + 20 | 36·6 | 172·1 | 5,939 |
| 13 | 216 | Sugar | + 20 | 18·5 | 81·6 | 5,792 |
| 26 | 274 | Paint and printing ink | + 17 | 48·0 | 90·9 | 5,654 |
| 14 | 217 | Cocoa, chocolate and sugar confectionery | + 16 | 99·0 | 88·2 | 5,473 |
| 127 | 709 | Miscellaneous transport services and storage | + 15 | 64·2 | 127·1 | 5,537 |
| 182 | 431 | Leather fellmongery | + 14 | 31·7 | 80·1 | 5,346 |
| 132 | 860 | Insurance, banking and finance | + 13 | 518·5 | 125·1 | 5,544 |
| 3 | 003 | Fishing | + 12 | 26·4 | 79·2 | 5,694 |
| 54 | 370/1 | Shipbuilding and repairing | + 12 | 202·3 | 76·1 | 5,602 |
| 75 | 417 | Hosiery and other knitted goods | + 11 | 115·6 | 109·8 | 5,799 |
| 33 | 321 | Light metals | + 8 | 57·0 | 102·9 | 5,590 |
| 134 | 872 | Educational services | + 2 | 846·9 | 150·3 | 5,059 |

| | | | | | | |
|---|---|---|---|---|---|---|
| 110 | 492 | Linoleum, leather cloth, etc. | 0 | 18·4 | 72·8 | 5,785 |
| 30 | 311 | Iron and steel (general) | — 2 | 277·7 | 100·5 | 5,625 |
| 108 | 489 | 'Other' printing, publishing, etc. | — 2 | 229·1 | 114·6 | 5,407 |
| 91 | 449 | Dress industries n.e.s. | — 3 | 39·9 | 93·3 | 5,429 |
| 6 | 103 | Chalk, clay, sand and gravel extraction | — 4 | 22·6 | 109·8 | 5,048 |
| 143 | 885 | Laundries | — 5 | 128·5 | 75·8 | 5,006 |
| 133 | 871 | Accountancy services | — 10 | 77·1 | 118·1 | 5,239 |
| 18 | 231 | Brewing and malting | — 13 | 95·0 | 93·8 | 5,111 |
| 15 | 218 | Fruit and vegetable products | — 16 | 72·0 | 99·9 | 5,226 |
| 55 | 370/2 | Marine engineering | — 17 | 75·6 | 50·8 | 5,731 |
| 129 | 820 | Retail distribution | — 18 | 1,805·5 | 101·2 | 5,128 |
| 32 | 313 | Iron castings, etc. | — 20 | 121·4 | 91·4 | 5,311 |
| 74 | 416 | Rope, twine and net | — 24 | 13·3 | 69·9 | 5,882 |
| 130 | 831 | Dealing in coal, materials, etc. | — 25 | 156·2 | 77·7 | 5,240 |
| 61 | 389 | Perambulators, hand trucks, etc. | — 27 | 7·5 | 71·4 | 5,757 |
| 104 | 481 | Paper and board | — 28 | 92·1 | 100·7 | 5,457 |
| 150 | 901 | National government service | — 29 | 299·7 | 106·7 | 5,464 |
| 2 | 002 | Forestry | — 32 | 20·5 | 72·6 | 4,845 |
| 10 | 213 | Biscuits | — 33 | 56·5 | 92·4 | 5,662 |
| 131 | 832 | Dealing in 'other' industrial materials | — 34 | 116·7 | 111·1 | 5,266 |
| 78 | 421 | Narrow fabrics | — 34 | 21·1 | 98·8 | 5,654 |
| 84 | 433 | Fur | — 34 | 8·9 | 87·6 | 5,957 |
| 135 | 873 | Legal services | — 35 | 82·9 | 131·3 | 5,256 |
| 146 | 888 | Repair of boots and shoes | — 36 | 18·2 | 51·1 | 5,321 |

| Project Code No. | Industry MLH No. | Industry | Change in Tress score | Total employment '000, 1959 | 1968 employment as % of 1959 | 1959 Tress score |
|---|---|---|---|---|---|---|
| 124 | 705 | Port and inland water transport | —41 | 152·4 | 88·2 | 5,609 |
| 47 | 352 | Watches and clocks | —41 | 14·8 | 93·7 | 5,824 |
| 137 | 875 | Religious organisations | —48 | 20·8 | 99·2 | 5,663 |
| 118 | 602 | Electricity | —52 | 207·1 | 118·0 | 5,007 |
| 126 | 707 | Postal services and telecommunications | —52 | 164·7 | 116·5 | 5,651 |
| 21 | 261 | Coke ovens and manufactured fuel | —52 | 19·8 | 83·7 | 5,638 |
| 1 | 001 | Agriculture and horticulture | —54 | 545·4 | 69·7 | 4,530 |
| 57 | 382 | Motor cycle, 3-wheel vehicle, pedal cycle | —59 | 36·6 | 62·3 | 5,906 |
| 149 | 899 | 'Other' services | —60 | 260·9 | 175·1 | 5,500 |
| 68 | 399 | Metal industries n.e.s. | —62 | 332·6 | 116·8 | 5,554 |
| 4 | 101 | Coal mining | —64 | 768·6 | 57·6 | 5,536 |
| 7 | 107 | 'Other' mining and quarrying | —68 | 16·2 | 68·6 | 5,576 |
| 8 | 211 | Grain milling | —72 | 40·7 | 90·4 | 4,977 |
| 117 | 601 | Gas | —81 | 132·4 | 95·6 | 5,299 |
| 29 | 277 | Polishes, gelatine, adhesives, etc. | —95 | 12·0 | 115·0 | 5,615 |
| 121 | 702 | Road passenger transport | —105 | 273·8 | 95·6 | 4,926 |
| 120 | 701 | Railways | —110 | 471·4 | 62·3 | 5,096 |
| 19 | 239 | 'Other' drink industries | —110 | 60·7 | 110·9 | 5,201 |
| 93 | 461 | Bricks, fireclay and refractory goods | —131 | 75·1 | 88·3 | 5,087 |

| 139 | 881 | Cinemas, theatres, radio, etc. | —172 | 141·7 | 87·8 | 5,351 |
| 35 | 331 | Agricultural machinery (excl. tractors) | —178 | 36·6 | 94·7 | 4,909 |
| 59 | 384 | Locomotives and railway track equipment | —189 | 71·8 | 38·9 | 5,555 |
| 60 | 385 | Railway carriages and wagons and trams | —212 | 78·4 | 40·5 | 5,336 |
| 142 | 884 | Catering, hotels, etc. | —218 | 565·2 | 102·6 | 5,198 |
| 147 | 889 | Hairdressing and manicure | —234 | 75·8 | 130·0 | 5,200 |
| 145 | 887 | Motor repairers, garages, etc. | —287 | 335·0 | 125·2 | 5,092 |
| 45 | 342/49 | Arms and engineering n.e.s. | —299 | 217·9 | 233·2 | 5,370 |
| 151 | 906 | Local government service | —361 | 736·3 | 114·6 | 5,025 |

**Table 4.5**  Summary of changes in Tress scores for Minimum List industries (1959 minus 1968)

| Quintile group, from positive change at top to negative at bottom | Primary 001–109 | Manufacturing 211–499 | Services 500–906 | Total |
|---|---|---|---|---|
| 1st | 0 | 27 | 4 | 31 |
| 2nd | 0 | 27 | 3 | 30 |
| 3rd | 1 | 23 | 6 | 30 |
| 4th | 3 | 18 | 9 | 30 |
| 5th | 3 | 13 | 15 | 31 |
| Total | 7 | 108 | 37 | 152 |

Source: Table 4.4

deviation are calculated separately for the two main groups of industries, the following picture emerges:

|  | Manufacturing industries | Service industries |
|---|---|---|
| Mean Tress change (1959 minus 1968) | +58·9 | —14·3 |
| Standard deviation | 99·9 | 141·5 |

Note that in calculating the mean change, each industry has been treated as of equal weight.

The figures in Table 4.4 were used to examine whether any explanation could be obtained for changes in the Tress score of industries. Of the three independent variables, the 1959 total employment proved to be quite unrelated to the dependent variable and hence the following equation was derived:

$$Y = -793 \cdot 922 + 0 \cdot 7081 X_1 + 0 \cdot 1373 X_2 \quad R^2 = 0 \cdot 160 \quad F = 14 \cdot 216$$

where $Y$ is the change in Tress score (1959 minus 1968), $X_1$ is the 1968 employment as a percentage of 1959 and $X_2$ is the 1959 Tress score. The result, acceptable at the 99 per cent level, shows that the greater the growth and the larger the 1959 Tress score, the greater the tendency to dispersion. However, with only 16 per cent

94

of the variance accounted for, the model is not very powerful.

An attempt was therefore made to see whether better results could be obtained by sub-dividing the data, using the same contingency table technique as was applied to the data in Table 4.1. However, this exercise did not lead to any improvement in the results and therefore confirmed that the equation reported above is probably the best that can be fitted.

The fact that the 1959 Tress score is one of the explanatory variables that can be accepted as significant shows that at the industry level, just as at the regional level, the gap between localised (specialised) and dispersed (diversified) patterns is closing.

### Conclusion

It must be admitted that the results reported in this chapter do not allow very firm conclusions to be drawn regarding the explanation of the patterns of industrial localisation that have been observed. There is clearly the important effect of transport costs upon the extent to which industries are localised or dispersed, and there does seem to be an overall tendency for industries to become more dispersed. This latter point is clearly consistent with our earlier finding that in general the employment structures of sub-divisions are becoming more diversified. However, and again consistent with previous findings, it is clear that there is some convergence of the extremes toward the mean level of dispersal. Finally, and perhaps most noteworthy, the manufacturing industries are more localised than the service industries and display a general tendency to greater dispersal, whereas the opposite trend appears to hold for services. This is again consistent with earlier findings regarding the structure of employment in the sub-regions. Thus the manufacturing and service sectors are converging toward the mean situation.

If the explanatory power of the available independent variables is low, then it seems clear that in future work a major effort must be made to obtain data on other variables that may be relevant. For example, it may be important to enquire into the structure of companies in the various industries, to establish the functional linkages both within industries and between them at the sub-regional level. Unfortunately, it was beyond our resources to pursue the enquiry thus far.

# Chapter 5 The Contribution of Industrial Change to Sub-Regional Growth

One of the main causes of regional disparities in growth and prosperity is the fact that in some areas the structure of employment includes a marked emphasis upon expanding trades whereas in other areas there is a noticeable concentration on slow growing or declining ones. This basic fact has been recognised for many years and may be termed the 'structural' element in regional and sub-regional growth. In recent years, however, there has been considerable interest in the related question of whether industries perform equally well in all parts of the country, i.e. the question of differential 'growth'. There has been considerable discussion of a technique for assessing these two components of regional growth, the technique known as shift-and-share (Chalmers, 1971, Paraskevopoulos, 1971; Bishop and Simpson, 1972).

When the work reported in this monograph was first being planned, it was intended to undertake a shift-and-share study. This would have been the first time such an exercise had been carried out for the whole country at the level of industrial and spatial disaggregation here employed. However, further consideration of the technique persuaded us that it is open to too many criticisms or, if not criticism, ambiguities of interpretation, for its use to be warranted with the data available to us. There are grave problems, as in all index number exercises, of choosing between or combining initial year and terminal year weights. Furthermore, should one use the sub-regional employment structure and apply to it the national rates of growth (or decline); or should one use the national employment structure and apply the sub-regional rates of growth? In principle, perhaps, it would be desirable to embark on a series of experiments in which the results from the various combinations and permutations could be compared. The magnitude of this task was a major deterrent. Another, and probably more important consideration, relates to a fundamental assumption of the shift-and-share technique.

It is a basic assumption of the technique that within a geographical area (sub-region in our case), the behaviour of one industry is independent of the behaviour of all others. Similarly, it is assumed that the behaviour of industry A in area 1 has no effect upon the experience of industry B in area 2. In other words, there are assumed to be no inter-industry and inter-area input-output relationships. Clearly, this is a nonsensical proposition in principle, though it may be justifiable as a working assumption if there is good reason for supposing that these inter-industry and inter-area relationships are of relatively small importance—as is probably the case when using the twenty-four SIC orders and the standard regions as the geographical units. However, with sixty-one sub-regions and 152 industries, it seemed intuitively obvious that the assumption of independence is untenable. Therefore, we did not embark upon a full shift-and-share analysis but contented ourselves with a rather humbler exercise.

### Contingency tables of industrial change

If we consider any one industry, it has spatially varied rates of change—either growth or decline in employment—which can be expressed as percentage change. But the absolute number of people involved also varies. Thus, a very high rate of growth from a miniscule base is not particularly significant or interesting, since it may reflect the activities of one plant and an increase in total employment from say 1 to 10; while dramatic in percentage terms, this is clearly unimportant in its impact on sub-regional employment. Therefore, we conceive of a contingency table, as illustrated in Figure 5.1. The square space is divided by two orthogonal axes, on both of which zero is at the intersection, on either side of which are negative and positive values. If the square represents a sub-region, then every industry can be given a unique location on the map, occupying a point in one of the quadrants. Thus, an industry that appears at the top left has experienced *both* a large percentage and also absolute decline in employment. The quadrants may be sub-divided either horizontally or vertically, so that one may distinguish industries with the following combinations of change:

1. Large positive percentage and large positive absolute change
2. Large negative percentage and large negative absolute change
3. Large positive percentage and low positive absolute change

4.  Large negative percentage and low negative absolute change
5.  Low positive percentage and high positive absolute change
6.  Low negative percentage and high negative absolute change

For the examination of the spatial structure of economic change, main interest attaches to items 1, 2, 5 and 6 above. In particular, which industries most commonly fall into these four categories and which sub-regions are most prominent in having them?

For operational purposes, the following procedures have been adopted. Each sub-region has been taken in turn and both the absolute and percentage change in employment in the 152 MLH industries calculated. This readily shows which changes are positive and which are negative. The sub-division into 'high' and 'low' change has been done as follows. In Figure 5.2 all industries with both a percentage and absolute change in excess of ±0·5 of one standard deviation are included. Referring back to Figure 5.1 the

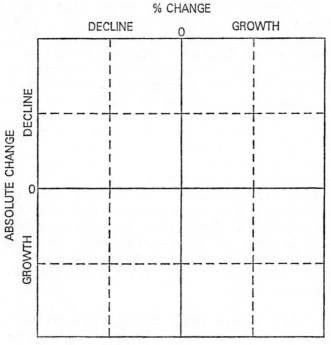

Fig. 5.1  Schematic contingency table.

pecked lines have been set at $\pm 0.5$ standard deviation and the two main axes at the respective mean values. Figure 5.2 thus shows the industries that occupy two corner sectors in each sub-region. On the other hand, in Figure 5.3 industries are shown with an average percentage change, defined as between $+0.5$ and $-0.5$ standard deviation, and an extreme absolute change of greater than $\pm 1.0$ standard deviation.

A word must be said about the calculation of percentage change. In all cases where there was zero employment in a sub-region, the nought was changed to one. This avoids the problem of dividing by or into nought. Secondly, the percentage change was allowed to reach but not to exceed 500 per cent. This device means that in the few cases where the very small absolute number employed had increased by an astronomical percentage the change was 'pegged' at 500 per cent. In this way, rather serious problems of weighting are avoided.

Figure 5.2 shows the array of industries which, in each of the sub-regions, had both a large percentage change and absolute change. If we deal with the declining employments first, the most striking point to note is the frequency with which industries *120* and *148* appear as important factors in the contraction of employment. The former (MLH 701, Railways) has had a dramatic and widespread decline in employment that has gone relatively unnoticed in recent years; the same is true of the mainly female employing industry *148* (MLH 891, Private domestic service). In both cases, these industries have had a bigger impact on employment levels than the much more generally recognised effects of the decline in Coal mining (*4*, MLH 101) and Shipbuilding and associated industries (*54* and *55*, MLH 370/1 and 370/2). Furthermore, whereas these last occur respectively in six and eleven sub-regions, industries *59* and *60* (MLH 384 and 385, Locomotives and railway track equipment, Railway carriages and wagons and trams) both appear in twelve sub-regions.

With respect to the rapidly growing industries, it is noticeable that again both manufacturing and service industries are important, but none of the primary industries. Among the manufacturing industries, *43*, *44* and *45* (MLH 339, 341, 342 and 349), a group of rather miscellaneous engineering activities, stand out as having geographically widespread growth. In the same category come *50*, *51*, *53*, *56*, *68*, *97* and *114*. Numbers *50* to *53*

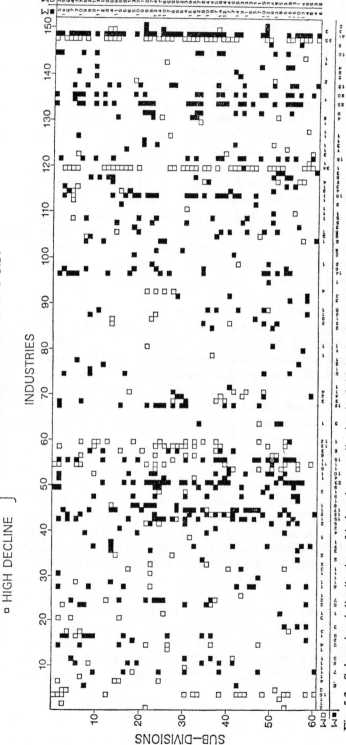

**Fig. 5.2** Sub-regional distribution of industries contributing both high absolute and high percentage change in employment, 1959–1968.

■ HIGH GROWTH

□ HIGH DECLINE

} in relative and absolute terms. ± ·5 S.D.

INDUSTRIES

SUB-DIVISIONS

are Electrical and electronic industries, including Domestic appliances (MLH 363, 364 and 369); 56 is the manufacture of Motor vehicles (MLH 381); 68 and 97 are Miscellaneous metal industries (MLH 399) and Miscellaneous building materials (MLH 469). Finally, 114 (MLH 496) is the moulding and fabricating of plastics. Apart from the manufacture of vehicles, which depends on a network of components suppliers, these growth industries are mainly characterised as being light, foot-loose industries, but heterogeneous in composition. Among the service employments, 149 (MLH 899, 'Other' services) is outstanding, having contributed substantial growth in no less than forty-one sub-regions. And whereas rail employment has generally declined, Road haulage contracting (122, MLH 703) has shown general growth, as have Educational services (134, MLH 872), Medical and dental services (136, MLH 874) and 'Other' professional and scientific services (138, MLH 879).

Figure 5.3 shows the distribution of industries contributing a large absolute change in employment but only a modest percentage growth or decline. With reference to the declining industries, it is striking that Agriculture and horticulture (1, MLH 001) is entered for forty sub-regions and that Coal mining again figures prominently. Altogether, the primary sector has been a significant source of employment decline in most sub-regions. Also striking is the appearance of industry 120 (MLH 701, Railways) in twenty-three sub-regions; as this industry appears in twenty-four of the sub-regions in Figure 5.2, altogether it contributes to substantial decline in fifty-seven out of the sixty-one sub-regions. Equally notable has been the widespread loss of work in industry 129 (MLH 820, Retail distribution) balanced by an equally widespread gain. Practically all the industries with widespread gain are in the service sector, the main industries being 116 (MLH 500, Construction), Educational services (124, MLH 872), Medical and dental services (136, MLH 874) and vehicle repair and servicing (145, MLH 887). It is particularly noteworthy that when Figures 5.2 and 5.3 are compared, it is evident that Educational services and Medical and dental services appear in fifty-seven and fifty-six sub-regions respectively.

A feature of both Figures 5.2 and 5.3 that is most striking is the way in which industries appear as contributing either to substantial growth *or* decline. In the great majority of cases, all

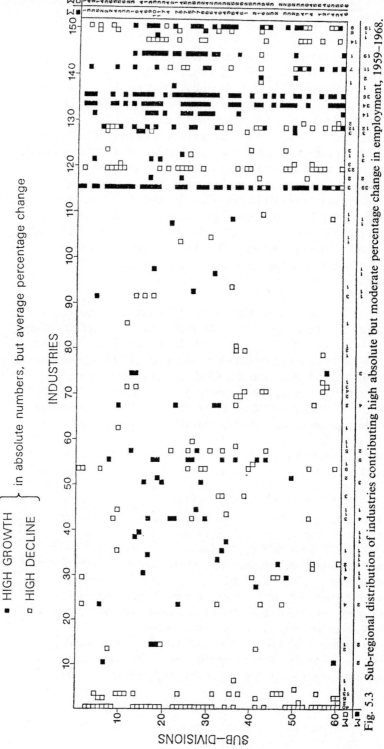

Fig. 5.3 Sub-regional distribution of industries contributing high absolute but moderate percentage change in employment, 1959–1968.

● HIGH GROWTH ⎫ in absolute numbers, but average percentage change
□ HIGH DECLINE ⎭

INDUSTRIES

SUB-DIVISIONS

the entries are in the growth or decline range or there is only the odd one or two against the general trend. In Figure 5.2, there are only two exceptions and neither is important. Figure 5.3, however, does contain two major examples contrary to this general rule— *129* (MLH 820, Retail distribution) and *142* (MLH 884, Catering, hotels, etc.). Thus, it seems reasonable to conclude that major growth or decline of an industry is much more conditioned by national factors affecting the structure of the economy than by the relative competitive power of the sub-regions.

Examination of the row totals in the two diagrams indicates the performance of the sub-regions It will be noted that in Figure 5.2 every sub-region has at least one industry in the category of high rate of decline and that in the majority of cases the number in this group is less than the number growing quickly. In Figure 5.3, however, there are some regions with an absence of either positive or negative entries and a large number in which the negative entries are more numerous than the positive ones—altogether twenty-five. The question does arise, therefore, whether some sub-regions have in fact had a better or worse growth performance than others, i.e. whether the conclusion stated at the end of the last paragraph, based on analysis at the industry level, is substantiated by analysis of the sub-regions. To pursue this question, the following hypothesis may be advanced. Those sub-regions that have been eligible for government aid are likely to have a relatively large number of industries identified in Figures 5.2 and 5.3 as declining. Conversely, areas that have not been assisted should have a preponderance of industries identified as growing. To examine this idea, the sub-regions were divided into three classes, as shown in Table 5.1, on the basis of the assistance index discussed in Chapter 3. Twenty-seven of the sub-regions have received no assistance and the remaining thirty-four were divided into two equal groups. For each of the three groups so identified, the mean number of growing and declining industries, and the standard deviations, were calculated.

Now it will be recollected that the assistance index did not perform very well as a variable to explain spatial patterns of change in diversification/specialisation. However, even though crude, it is a reasonable way of classifying the sub-regions according to the extent of the 'perceived' regional problem. Thus, it is quite striking that the differences between the mean values

**Table 5.1** The number of growing and declining industries in the sub-regions

| Assistance Index | Growth industries | | Declining industries | |
|---|---|---|---|---|
| | *Mean number* | *S.D.* | *Mean number* | *S.D.* |
| No assistance | 13·6 | 3·1 | 7·8 | 2·8 |
| 0·0—37·0 | 12·4 | 3·5 | 7·5 | 2·6 |
| 37·0 and over | 11·4 | 4·2 | 7·4 | 2·7 |

Sources: 5.2 and 5.3

shown in Table 5.1 are so small: indeed, they are too small to be regarded as significant. The implication is clear. The persistence of high unemployment levels and the other symptoms of regional imbalance is *not* due to the industries that may be regarded as the 'commanding heights' of the sub-regional economies but arises from the collective performance of the minor industries. From this, it is clear that the problem of regional imbalance relates to considerations that are diffused among many industries. This may explain the apparently limited effects of government policies in affecting industrial structure.

These results are in partial conflict with the findings of other workers, notably Humphrys (1962). He took the period 1951 to 1960, the twenty-four SIC Orders and eleven standard regions covering the whole of Great Britain. Interest was focused on growth industries which were defined as growing faster than the average for all those industries which experienced growth in employment, i.e. in excess of 12 per cent in the ten-year period. The six industries so defined accounted for 78 per cent of all employment increase in the growing industries. Humphrys came to the conclusion 'that there is little relationship between the location of an industry and the rate at which it grows' (p.55), though he qualified this conclusion as follows:

'The highest rate of growth in all the growth industries is to be found in a region south east of the Humber-Mersey line, though the lowest rate of increase is also to be found there in two instances . . . Scotland is above average in only one instance—Insurance—and actually showed a decline in one—Vehicles. The South East part of Britain is then the favoured area, as regards both the location of the growth industries and their growth rates, and Scotland seems to be least favoured in both cases.' (Humphrys, 1962, p.54)

Granted the difference in time period and level of aggregation both spatially and by sector, the evidence from our study is more consistent with the first conclusion quoted than with the tenor of the longer passage. Our evidence is much more indicative of geographically widespread growth (or decline) and throws doubt on the commonly accepted belief in the advantages of metropolitan and midland England. Indeed, the results reported here are consistent with Stilwell's (1969) conclusion that over the period 1959 to 1967, the industrial composition of employment in Wales, the Northern and North-Western standard regions changed in a manner favourable to faster growth, while the reverse occurred in the East Midlands, in Yorkshire and Humberside and in the South-East region.

**Conclusion**

The main conclusion to be drawn from the evidence cited in this chapter, is the way in which industries tend to appear in Figures 5.2 and 5.3 as either growing or declining. This implies that the performance of an industry is affected by national considerations much more than by local ones. This conclusion is confirmed by the data in Table 5.1 for the sub-regions. It seems to follow that the poor performance of some sub-regions relative to others is due to the behaviour of the minor industries, and this probably means that complex questions of inter-industry linkages at the local level are of great importance. But if this is indeed the case, then it is abundantly clear that a much more sophisticated approach to regional policy is necessary than has hitherto been manifest.

# Chapter 6 Conclusion

In one sense, the results reported in this book are disappointing; in another, they are provocative and exciting. Disappointment lies in the fact that only a low level of statistical rigour has been feasible in our analyses and that we have had only mediocre success in explaining the patterns that have been described. The converse of this proposition, however, is that a whole range of intriguing problems is left asked but unanswered. In a nutshell, the main hypothesis advanced in Chapter 1, that the assisted areas should display the greatest diversification of employment has not found support. On the other hand, alternative explanations of the observed phenomena have accounted for only a small part of the variance.

Perhaps the main conclusions to emerge from this study lie outside the issues that have been specifically discussed. In his 1972 book on regional economics in Britain, Brown asks the question: how should regions be defined?, and affirms in reply that 'how one delimits regions should depend on the purpose for which one does it' (p.27). In practice, he then proceeds to use the standard regions, for the very good reason that it is for these areas that most data are available. Concerned with inter-regional economic and social differences, Brown does not enquire whether these inter-regional variations are greater or less than intra-regional differences. The material that we have presented indicates clearly two points relevant in this context. In the first place, the standard regions are far from homogeneous, a fact familiar to geographers for a long time. More important, and less obvious, there are spatial patterns that cut across the framework of the standard regions. In this respect, the present study complements the work of Chisholm and O'Sullivan (1973). They used freight flow data for seventy-eight zones covering Great Britain, and so were working with a level of spatial disaggregation comparable to that employed in the present study.

The economic planning sub-regions can lay no claim to being perfect units for analysis and, therefore, it would be improper to over-emphasise the deficiencies of studies based on the standard regions. What does now seem to be established is the need for careful experiment as to which is the best level of aggregation to employ in a given context. And this need is all the more urgent the nearer any study approaches to policy prescription. But however important it may be to do this kind of exercise, the lack of data for units smaller than standard regions is a serious impediment. Another obstacle is, of course, the sheer volume of work involved in handling data sets even for sixty-odd areas, let alone larger numbers.

In the context of the above discussion, it seems abundantly clear that the low level of explanation that we have achieved is not an indication that the sponge has been squeezed dry but rather reflects the poverty of data on variables that are likely to be relevant. We would argue, therefore, that our results indicate strongly the need for much better statistical information for geographical units smaller than standard regions.

Let us now turn to our specific findings. In the first place, we have found that between 1959 and 1968 the trend that had been noted by other workers for both before and after the last war, toward the diversification of employment, has been maintained. However, there are important areas where the opposite has been happening—notably London and its environs, Birmingham and Merseyside and other pockets fairly generally scattered over the country. Equally important, diversification has been a feature of employment in manufacturing but not in the service trades, where indeed the opposite tendency has predominated. In fact, rather than a general tendency to diversification it is perhaps more relevant to stress the convergence of employment structures towards the national mean, with a slight trend to overall diversification. This convergence process seems to be sufficiently strong to mask any effects of government policy that might be detected, as hypothesised in Chapter 1. As a result, no evidence could be found to support the proposition that government policies in aid of the assisted areas have in fact resulted in a disproportionately rapid diversification in these areas. In this respect, therefore, we do not have tangible evidence by which to measure the success or otherwise of government policies.

One of the less expected but potentially more important results is that the level of diversification in an area of given total employment is tending to increase rather than decrease. This

107

finding runs counter to *a priori* expectations based on the notion of scale economies increasing over time and indeed the empirical fact that manufacturing plants are getting larger. If this trend to greater local diversity of employment for a given total number of employees is maintained, it may have important repercussions for the stability of job opportunities in the smaller sub-regions.

Just as the sub-regions are in general diversifying, so industries are generally becoming less localised. But it is noteworthy that whereas the manufacturing industries are dispersing the service trades are becoming more localised. This may have important implications for regional policies, in that the service sector is the most rapidly growing provider of employment. Thus, if these industries become more highly localised, then there may be trouble in the future if the number of workers they employ should decline. There would then be all the difficulties of structural adaptation in the face of secular employment decline that have plagued parts of Britain during the last few decades.

It is also of considerable interest that industries showing marked growth are not localised in only some sub-regions: also that declining industries are fairly generally spread. Indeed, the evidence in Chapter 5 does not lend support to the notion that some regions have a generally good or bad growth history for major sources of employment. So far as some areas have performed well or badly, it would appear that fairly complex patterns of inter-industry linkages must be sought for. Such a conclusion would certainly reinforce any doubts that one may have about the utility of the shift-and-share mode of analysis.

Thus, at the end of the day, the reader is invited to regard the present book as an exploration, almost a reconnaissance, that has thrown up far more questions than we have been able to answer. We offer our results as a modest contribution to an important debate on the way the space-economy does actually work and may be influenced by official policy. We certainly hope that others will carry the discussion forward.

# Appendix

# Numbers allocated to sub-regions for the purpose of the present study

**Northern Region**

| | |
|---|---|
| Industrial North East, North | 01 |
| „        „       „    South | 02 |
| Rural North East, North | |
| „        „       „    South | 04 |
| Cumberland & Westmorland | 05 |

**Yorks. and Humberside Region**

| | |
|---|---|
| North Humberside | 06 |
| South        „ | 07 |
| Mid Yorkshire | 08 |
| South Lindsey | 09 |
| South Yorkshire | 10 |
| Yorkshire Coalfield | 11 |
| West Yorkshire | 12 |

**East Midlands Region**

| | |
|---|---|
| Nottingham/Derbyshire | 13 |
| Leicester | 14 |
| Eastern Lowlands | 15 |
| Northampton | 16 |

**East Anglia Region**

| | |
|---|---|
| South East | 17 |
| North East | 18 |
| North West | 19 |
| South West | 20 |

**South East Region**

| | |
|---|---|
| Greater London | 21 |
| Outer Metropolitan | 22 |
| Outer South East: | |
| Essex | 23 |
| Kent | 24 |
| Sussex Coast | 25 |
| Solent | 26 |

| | |
|---|---|
| Beds, Berks, Bucks, and Oxford | 27 |

**South West Region**

| | |
|---|---|
| Central | 28 |
| Southern | 29 |
| Western | 30 |
| Northern | 31 |

**West Midlands Region**

| | |
|---|---|
| Central | 32 |
| Conurbation | 33 |
| Coventry Belt | 34 |
| The Rural West | 35 |
| North Staffs | 36 |

**North West Region**

| | |
|---|---|
| South Cheshire (High Peak) | 37 |
| South Lancs | 38 |
| Manchester | 39 |
| Merseyside | 40 |
| Furness | 41 |
| Fylde | 42 |
| Lancaster | 43 |
| Mid Lancs | 44 |
| North East Lancs | 45 |

**Wales**

| | |
|---|---|
| Industrial South Wales: | |
| C & E Valleys | 46 |
| W-S Wales | 47 |
| Coastal Belt | 48 |
| North East Wales | 49 |
| North Coast | 50 |
| N-W Wales: Remainder | 51 |
| Central Wales | 52 |
| South West Wales | 53 |

## Scotland

*Note:* these sub-regions are shown in the outline map on page 110.

# Minimum List industries

| INDUSTRY | Minimum List Heading | Code number used in the study |
|---|---|---|
| **Agriculture, Forestry, Fishing** | | |
| Agriculture and Horticulture | 001 | 1 |
| Forestry | 002 | 2 |
| Fishing | 003 | 3 |
| **Mining and Quarrying** | | |
| Coal Mining | 101 | 4 |
| Stone and Slate Quarrying and Mining | 102 | 5 |
| Chalk, Clay, Sand and Gravel Extraction | 103 | 6 |
| Other Mining and Quarrying | 109 | 7 |
| **Food, Drink and Tobacco** | | |
| Grain Milling | 211 | 8 |
| Bread and Flour Confectionery | 212 | 9 |
| Biscuits | 213 | 10 |
| Bacon Curing, Meat and Fish Products | 214 | 11 |
| Milk Products | 215 | 12 |
| Sugar | 216 | 13 |
| Cocoa, Chocolate and Sugar Confectionery | 217 | 14 |
| Fruit and Vegetable Products | 218 | 15 |
| Animal and Poultry Foods | 219 | 16 |
| Food Industries not elsewhere specified | 229 | 17 |
| Brewing and Malting | 231 | 18 |
| Other Drink Industries | 239 | 19 |
| Tobacco | 240 | 20 |
| **Chemicals and Allied Industries** | | |
| Coke Ovens and Manufactured Fuel | 261 | 21 |
| Mineral Oil Refining | 262 | 22 |
| Lubricating Oils and Greases | 263 | 23 |
| Chemicals & Dyes, Explosives & Fireworks | 271/73 | 24 |
| Pharmaceutical and Toilet Preparations | 272 | 25 |
| Paint and Printing Ink | 274 | 26 |

TCPOE–H

| INDUSTRY | Minimum List Heading | Code number used in the study |
|---|---|---|
| **Chemicals and Allied Industries**—*cont'd* | | |
| Vegetable and Animal Oils, Fats, Soap and | | |
| Detergents | 275 | 27 |
| Synthetic Resins and Plastics Materials | 276 | 28 |
| Polishes, Gelatine, Adhesives, etc. | 277 | 29 |
| | | |
| **Metal Manufacture** | | |
| Iron and Steel (General) | 311 | 30 |
| Steel Tubes | 312 | 31 |
| Iron Castings, etc. | 313 | 32 |
| Light Metals | 321 | 33 |
| Copper, Brass and Other Base Metals | 322 | 34 |
| | | |
| **Engineering and Electrical Goods** | | |
| Agricultural Machinery (Except Tractors) | 331 | 35 |
| Metal-Working Machine Tools | 332 | 36 |
| Engineers' Small Tools and Gauges | 333 | 37 |
| Industrial Engines | 334 | 38 |
| Textile Machinery and Accessories | 335 | 39 |
| Contractors' Plant and Quarrying | | |
| Machinery | 336 | 40 |
| Mechanical Handling Equipment | 337 | 41 |
| Office Machinery | 338 | 42 |
| Other Machinery | 339 | 43 |
| Industrial Plant and Steelwork | 341 | 44 |
| Ordnance and Small Arms, Other | | |
| Mechanical Engineering not elsewhere | | |
| specified | 342/49 | 45 |
| Scientific, Surgical and Photographic | | |
| Instruments, etc. | 351 | 46 |
| Watches and Clocks | 352 | 47 |
| Electrical Machinery | 361 | 48 |
| Insulated Wires and Cables | 362 | 49 |
| Telegraph and Telephone Apparatus | 363 | 50 |
| Radio and Other Electronic Apparatus | 364 | 51 |

| INDUSTRY | Minimum List Heading | Code number used in the study |
|---|---|---|
| **Engineering and Electrical Goods**—*cont'd.* | | |
| Domestic Electric Appliances | 365 | 52 |
| Other Electrical Goods | 369 | 53 |
| **Shipbuilding and Marine Engineering** | | |
| Shipbuilding and Ship-Repairing | 370/1 | 54 |
| Marine Engineering | 370/2 | 55 |
| **Vehicles** | | |
| Motor Vehicle Manufacturing | 381 | 56 |
| Motor Cycle, Three-Wheel Vehicle and Pedal Cycle Manufacturing | 382 | 57 |
| Aircraft Manufacturing and Repairing | 383 | 58 |
| Locomotives and Railway Track Equipment | 384 | 59 |
| Railway Carriages and Wagons and Trams | 385 | 60 |
| Perambulators, Hand Trucks, etc. | 389 | 61 |
| **Metal Goods not Elsewhere Specified** | | |
| Tools and Implements | 391 | 62 |
| Cutlery | 392 | 63 |
| Bolts, Nuts, Screws, Rivets, etc. | 393 | 64 |
| Wire and Wire Manufactures | 394 | 65 |
| Cans and Metal Boxes | 395 | 66 |
| Jewellery, Plate and Refining of Precious metals | 396 | 67 |
| Metal Industries not elsewhere specified | 399 | 68 |
| **Textiles** | | |
| Production of Man-Made Fibres | 411 | 69 |
| Spinning and Doubling of Cotton, Flax and Man-Made Fibres | 412 | 70 |
| Weaving of Cotton, Linen and Man-Made Fibres | 413 | 71 |
| Woollen and Worsted | 414 | 72 |
| Jute | 415 | 73 |
| Rope, Twine and Net | 416 | 74 |

| INDUSTRY | Minimum List Heading | Code number used in the study |
|---|---|---|
| **Textiles**—*cont'd* | | |
| Hosiery and other Knitted Goods | 417 | 75 |
| Lace | 418 | 76 |
| Carpets | 419 | 77 |
| Narrow Fabrics | 421 | 78 |
| Made-up Textiles | 422 | 79 |
| Textile Finishing | 423 | 80 |
| Other Textile Industries | 429 | 81 |
| | | |
| **Leather, Leather Goods and Fur** | | |
| Leather (Tanning and Dressing) and Fellmongery | 431 | 82 |
| Leather Goods | 432 | 83 |
| Fur | 433 | 84 |
| | | |
| **Clothing and Footwear** | | |
| Weatherproof Outerwear | 441 | 85 |
| Men's and Boys' Tailored Outerwear | 442 | 86 |
| Women's and Girls' Tailored Outerwear | 443 | 87 |
| Overalls and Men's Shirts, Underwear, etc. | 444 | 88 |
| Dresses, Lingerie, Infants' Wear, etc. | 445 | 89 |
| Hats, Caps and Millinery | 446 | 90 |
| Dress Industries not elsewhere specified | 449 | 91 |
| Footwear | 450 | 92 |
| | | |
| **Bricks, Pottery, Glass, Cement, etc.** | | |
| Bricks, Fireclay and Refractory Goods | 461 | 93 |
| Pottery | 462 | 94 |
| Glass | 463 | 95 |
| Cement | 464 | 96 |
| Abrasives and Building Materials, etc. not elsewhere specified | 469 | 97 |
| | | |
| **Timber, Furniture, etc.** | | |
| Timber | 471 | 98 |
| Furniture and Upholstery | 472 | 99 |

| INDUSTRY | Minimum List Heading | Code number used in the study |
|---|---|---|
| **Timber, Furniture, etc.**—*cont'd* | | |
| Bedding, etc. | 473 | 100 |
| Shop and Office Fitting | 474 | 101 |
| Wooden Containers and Baskets | 475 | 102 |
| Miscellaneous Wood and Cork Manufacturers | 479 | 103 |
| **Paper, Printing and Publishing** | | |
| Paper and Board | 481 | 104 |
| Cardboard Boxes, Cartons and Fibre-Board Packing Cases | 482 | 105 |
| Manufactures of Paper and Board not elsewhere specified | 483 | 106 |
| Printing, Publishing of Newspapers and Periodicals | 486 | 107 |
| Other Printing, Publishing, Bookbinding Engraving, etc. | 489 | 108 |
| **Other Manufacturing Industries** | | |
| Rubber | 491 | 109 |
| Linoleum, Leather Cloth, etc. | 492 | 110 |
| Brushes and Brooms | 493 | 111 |
| Toys, Games and Sports Equipment | 494 | 112 |
| Miscellaneous Stationers' Goods | 495 | 113 |
| Plastics Moulding and Fabricating | 496 | 114 |
| Miscellaneous Manufacturing Industries | 499 | 115 |
| **Construction** | 500 | 116 |
| **Gas, Electricity and Water** | | |
| Gas | 601 | 117 |
| Electricity | 602 | 118 |
| Water Supply | 603 | 119 |
| **Transport and Communication** | | |
| Railways | 701 | 120 |
| Road Passenger Transport | 702 | 121 |

| INDUSTRY | Minimum List Heading | Code number used in the study |
|---|---|---|
| **Transport and Communication**—*cont'd* | | |
| Road Haulage Contracting | 703 | 122 |
| Sea Transport | 704 | 123 |
| Port and Inland Water Transport | 705 | 124 |
| Air Transport | 706 | 125 |
| Postal Services and Telecommunications | 707 | 126 |
| Miscellaneous Transport Services and Storage | 709 | 127 |
| | | |
| **Distributive Trades** | | |
| Wholesale Distribution | 810 | 128 |
| Retail Distribution | 820 | 129 |
| Dealing in Coal, Builders' Materials, Grain and Agricultural Supplies (Wholesale or Retail) | 831 | 130 |
| Dealing in other Industrial Materials and Machinery | 832 | 131 |
| | | |
| **Insurance, Banking and Finance** | 860 | 132 |
| | | |
| **Professional and Scientific Services** | | |
| Accountancy Services | 871 | 133 |
| Educational Services | 872 | 134 |
| Legal Services | 873 | 135 |
| Medical and Dental Services | 874 | 136 |
| Religious Organisations | 875 | 137 |
| Other Professional and Scientific Services | 879 | 138 |
| | | |
| **Miscellaneous Services** | | |
| Cinemas, Theatres, Radio, etc. | 881 | 139 |
| Sport and Other Recreations | 882 | 140 |
| Betting | 883 | 141 |
| Catering, Hotels, etc. | 884 | 142 |
| Laundries | 885 | 143 |

| INDUSTRY | Minimum List Heading | Code number used in the study |
|---|---|---|
| **Miscellaneous Services**—*cont'd* | | |
| Dry Cleaning, Job Dyeing, Carpet Beating, etc. | 886 | 144 |
| Motor Repairers, Distributors, Garages and Filling Stations | 887 | 145 |
| Repair of Boots and Shoes | 888 | 146 |
| Hairdressing and Manicure | 889 | 147 |
| Private Domestic Service | 891 | 148 |
| Other Services | 899 | 149 |
| | | |
| **Public Administration** | | |
| National Government Service | 901 | 150 |
| Local Government Service | 906 | 151 |
| | | |
| **Ex-Service Personnel** | | 152 |

*N.B.* The category 'Others not classified by industry' is included in 152 for Greater London only.

# References

Bain, J. S. (1966). *International Differences in Industrial Structure. Eight Nations in the 1950s,* Yale University Press.

Bassett, K. and P. Haggett (1971). 'Towards short-term forecasting for cyclic behaviour in a regional system of cities', in M. Chisholm, A. E. Frey and P. Haggett (eds), *Regional Forecasting,* Butterworths, 389–413.

Bishop, K. C. and C. E. Simpson (1972). 'Components of change analysis: problems of alternative approaches to industrial structure', *Regional Studies,* 6, 59–68.

Britton, J. N. H. (1967). *Regional Analysis and Economic Geography. A case study of manufacturing in the Bristol region,* Bell.

Brown, A. J. (1969). 'Surveys of applied economics: regional economics, with special reference to the United Kingdom', *Economic Journal,* LXXIX, 759–96.

Brown, A. J. (1972). *The Framework of Regional Economics in the United Kingdom,* Cambridge University Press.

Chalmers, J. A. (1971). 'Measuring changes in regional industrial structure: a comment on Stilwell and Ashby', *Urban Studies,* 8, 289–92.

Chisholm, M. (1962). 'Location of industry', *Planning,* XXVIII, 466, Political and Economic Planning, 325–63.

Chisholm, M. (1968). *Rural Settlement and Land Use: an essay in location,* Hutchinson.

Chisholm, M. (1970). *Geography and Economics,* Bell.

Chisholm, M. and G. Manners (1971). 'Geographical space: a new dimension of public concern and policy', in M. Chisholm and G. Manners (eds), *Spatial Policy Problems of the British Economy,* Cambridge University Press, 1–23.

Chisholm, M. and P. O'Sullivan (1973). *Freight Flows and Spatial Aspects of the British Economy,* Cambridge University Press.

Clemente, F. and R. B. Sturgis (1971). 'Population size and industrial diversification', *Urban Studies,* 8, 65–8.

Conkling, E. C. (1964). 'The measurement of diversification', in G. Manners (ed), *South Wales in the Sixties. Studies in industrial geography,* Pergamon, 161–83.

Cunningham, N. J. (1970). 'The pattern of Merseyside employment 1949–66', in R. Lawton and M. Cunningham (eds), *Merseyside: social and economic studies*, Longman, 374–410.

Davies, H. W. E. and D. F. Hagger (1964). 'Aspects of the geography of employment', in G. Manners (ed), *South Wales in the Sixties. Studies in industrial geography*, Pergamon, 129–59.

Department of the Environment (1972). *Statistics for Town and Country Planning. Series II Floor Space. No. 2. Floor space in industrial, etc., shopping and office use. Total stock as at 1 April and changes April 1967 to March 1968*, H.M.S.O.

Edwards, S. L. (1970). 'Transport cost in British industry', *Journal of Transport Economics and Policy*, IV, 1–19.

Evely, R. and I. M. D. Little (1960). *Concentration in British Industry: an empirical study of the structure of industrial production, 1935–51*, Cambridge University Press.

Ferguson, A. G. and P. C. Forer (1973). 'Aspects of measuring employment specialization in Great Britain', *Area*, 5, 121–8.

Florence, P. S. (1944). 'The selection of industries suitable for dispersion into rural areas, *Journal*, Royal Statistical Society, CVII, 93–107.

Florence, P. S. (1962). *Post-War Investment, Location and Size of Plant*, Cambridge University Press.

Fuchs, V. R. (1962). *Changes in the Location of Manufacturing in the United States since 1929*, Yale University Press.

Gujarati, D. (1972). 'The behaviour of unemployment and unfilled vacancies: Great Britain, 1958–1971', *Economic Journal*, 82, 195–204.

Hall, P. G. (1962). *The Industries of London since 1861*, Hutchinson.

Hart, P. E. (1971). 'Entropy and other measures of concentration', *Journal*, Royal Statistical Society, 134, 73–85.

Hoover, E. M. (1971). *An Introduction to Regional Economics*, Alfred A. Knopf.

Horowitz, I. (1970). 'Employment concentration in the Common Market: an entropy approach', *Journal*, Royal Statistical Society, 133, 463–79.

Howard, R. S. (1968). *The Movement of Manufacturing Industry in the United Kingdom 1945–65*, Board of Trade, H.M.S.O.

Humphrys, G. (1962). 'Growth industries and the regional economies of Britain', *District Bank Review*, December, 35–56.

Isard, W. *et al* (1960). *Methods of Regional Analysis: an introduction to regional science*, M.I.T. Press.

Keeble, D. E. and D. P. Hauser (1971). 'Spatial analysis of manufacturing growth in outer south-east England 1960–1967. I Hypotheses and variables', *Regional Studies*, 5, 229–62.

Keeble, D. E. and D. H. Hauser (1972). 'Spatial analysis of manufacturing growth in outer south-east England 1960–1967. II Method and results', *Regional Studies*, 6, 11–36.

Kershaw, D. (1971). *Diversification of Industry in Britain*, undergraduate project submitted in part-fulfilment of the B.Sc. requirements, Department of Geography, University of Bristol.

Leser, C. E. V. (1948). 'Industrial specialisation in Scotland and in regions of England and Wales', *Yorkshire Bulletin of Economic and Social Research*, 1, 19–30.

Lloyd, P. E. (1970). 'The impact of Development Area policies on Merseyside 1949–1967', in R. Lawton and M. Cunningham (eds) *Merseyside: social and economic studies*, Longman, 374–410.

McCrone, G. (1969). *Regional Policy in Britain*, Allen and Unwin.

Ministry of Housing and Local Government (1969). *Statistics for Town and Country Planning. Series II Floor Space. No. 1 Floor space in industrial, shopping and office use. Changes April 1964 to March 1967*, H.M.S.O.

Paraskevopoulos, C. C. (1971). 'The stability of the regional-share component: an empirical test', *Journal of Regional Science*, 11, 107–112.

Rodgers, A. (1955). 'Some aspects of industrial diversification in the United States', *Papers and Proceedings*, Regional Science Association, *1*, 31–46.

Royal Commission (1940). *Royal Commission on the Distribution of the Industrial Population. Report*. Cmd. 6153.

Sant, M.E.C. (1971). *The Geography of Business Cycles: a case study of economic fluctuations in East Anglia, 1951–1968*, Ph.D. thesis, University of London.

Siegel, S. (1956). *Nonparametric Statistics for the Behavioral Sciences*, McGraw-Hill.

Smith, D. M. (1969). *Industrial Britain: the North West*, David and Charles.

Smith, W. (1949). *An Economic Geography of Great Britain*, Methuen.

Smith, W. (ed) (1953). *Scientific Survey of Merseyside*, University of Liverpool Press.

South East Economic Planning Council (1970). *South East Study of sub-divisions*, South East Economic Planning Council.

Steed, G. P. F. and M. D. Thomas (1971). 'Regional industrial change: Northern Ireland', *Annals*, Association of American Geographers, 61, 344–60.

Stilwell, F. J. B. (1969). 'Regional growth and structural adaptation', *Urban Studies*, 6, 162–78.

Theil, H. (1967). *Economics and Information Theory*, North-Holland.

Thompson, W. R. (1965). 'Urban economic growth and development in a national system of cities', in P. M. Hauser and L. F. Schnore, *The Study of Urbanization*, Wiley, 431–90.

Tress, R. C. (1938). 'Unemployment and the diversification of industry, *Manchester School*, IX, 140–52

# Index

Note that information shown in the Figures and Tables is not included in this Index, which refers only to the text.

For Product Safety Concerns and Information please contact our
EU representative GPSR@taylorandfrancis.com Taylor & Francis
Verlag GmbH, Kaufingerstraße 24, 80331 München, Germany